P9-CCQ-562

BEADWEAVING

BEADWEAVING

New Needle Techniques
& Original Designs

Ann Benson

A **Sterling/Chapelle Book**
Sterling Publishing Co., Inc. New York

Library of Congress Cataloging-in-Publication Data

Benson, Ann.
    Beadweaving : new needle techniques & original designs / by Ann
Benson.
        p.   cm.
    "A Sterling/Chapelle book."
    Includes index.
    ISBN 0-8069-0400-3
    1. Beadwork.   2. Jewelry making.   I. Title.
TT860.B47   1993   93-12799
745.58'2—dc20   CIP

10 9 8 7 6

A Sterling / Chapelle Book

Published by Sterling Publishing Company, Inc.
387 Park Avenue South, New York, N.Y. 10016
© 1993 by Chapelle Ltd.
Distributed in Canada by Sterling Publishing
$^{c}/o$ Canadian Manda Group, P.O. Box 920, Station U
Toronto, Ontario, Canada M8Z 5P9
Distributed in Great Britain and Europe by Cassell PLC
Villiers House, 41/47 Strand, London WC2N 5JE, England
Distributed in Australia by Capricorn Link Ltd.
P.O. Box 665, Lane Cove, NSW 2066
Printed and bound in Hong Kong
All rights reserved

Sterling ISBN 0-8069-0400-3

Chapelle Ltd.

Owners:
Jo Packham and Terrece Beesley

Staff:
Trice Boerens
Tina Annette Brady
, Sheri Lynn Castle
, Holly Fuller
Kristi Glissmeyer
Cherie Hanson
Susan Jorgensen
Margaret Shields Marti
Jackie McCowen
Barbara Milburn
Kathleen R. Montoya
Pamela Randall
Jennifer Roberts
Florence Stacey
Lew Stoddard
Nancy Whitley
Gloria Zirkel

Photographer:
Ryne Hazen

*This book is dedicated to my beloved daughters,
Meryl Glassman and Ariel Glassman.
It's such a treat to be your mother!*

Ann Benson is a well-known designer specializing in beaded jewelry and needlearts. In addition to designing many craft and needleart publications, she also co-authors several board games.

When Ann is not designing her beautiful beaded creations, she enjoys choral singing, bicycling and interior carpentry.

Miss Benson resides with her family in Amherst, Massachusetts.

CONTENTS

Chapter One

BEAD NEEDLEWEAVING GENERAL INSTRUCTIONS

Getting Started

Basic needleweaving may remind you of crocheting. The first row is worked, then subsequent rows are looped into the first row in a predictable way. Unlike crochet, which is usually worked from written directions, bead needleweaving is worked from a gridded pattern (except when weaving a sphere, which is worked from written directions).

Vertical rows of counted beads are attached to the previous vertical rows by a series of evenly-spaced loops. The ideal pattern is to loop after every third bead. In some cases, where great strength is needed, you may want to loop more frequently.

The first few rows are somewhat unstable and may seem difficult to work. Tricks for dealing with this temporary instability are described on the following pages. Be patient! After two or three rows, the weaving will be quite easy to handle.

Gather together your materials and tools, follow the step-by-step instructions, and enjoy!

Needles

Because of their great length, traditional beading needles are not well suited for needleweaving. A #9 embroidery needle is ideal when working with seed beads size 11 or larger. For some finely drilled stones and pearls, a #10 quilting needle is recommended.

Thread Types

Ordinary mercerized cotton sewing thread is recommended for most needleweaving. Choose a neutral color that is similar in theme to your bead design. It is nearly impossible to weave without a little thread showing between the beads, so try to minimize the distraction by using compatible thread.

Light nylon may be used, but it has greater bulk than ordinary sewing thread and should be restricted to uses where strength is a consideration. If you are using a lot of valuable stones or your beadweaving piece is supporting any weight, nylon may be a necessary choice.

Fine silk or cotton embroidery floss are good choices for use in needleweaving. Separate the plies of cotton 6-ply embroidery floss and use only one ply at a time.

Metallic threads are not recommended because the surface fiber tends to fray and ravel. When pulling metallic thread through a tight fitting bead, fibers will bunch up around the bead opening.

Thread Hints

Soaping or waxing the thread keeps it from tangling. Run the thread across the surface of the soap or wax, then pull the thread between your fingertips to remove any excess.

Adding a New Thread

When about 3" of thread remains unbeaded on the needle, it is time to add a new thread. Remove the needle from the old thread and cut a new 30" length. A longer piece will tend to tangle, and a shorter piece will require frequent additions of thread.

Tie a square knot so that the knot lands about 1" from where the old thread emerges from the beadwork; see Diagram A. Place a tiny dot of glue on the knot. Wipe off any excess glue, but you don't need to wait for the glue to dry before proceeding.

Continue beading as if you were using one continuous thread. Let the thread ends protrude from the work until the new thread is well established within the weave; see Diagram A. Then, pull gently on the ends and clip them close so they disappear into the weave. You may find it necessary to use a smaller needle until you have passed the area of the knot.

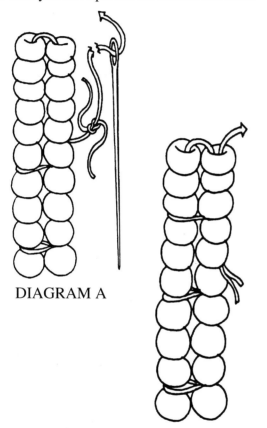

DIAGRAM A

About Beads

Although most beads are machine manufactured, it is essentially a hand-making process. There is a tremendous amount of variation from one bead to the next in each of the standard bead sizes. These odd-shaped beads can be beneficial and charming when used in some designs. However, to avoid frustration, when the hole in a bead is so tight it does not slip easily over the needle, discard it.

Removing Unwanted Beads

If you wish to remove beads from a row in which the looping is nearly complete, break them off with a medium-sized, all-purpose pliers.

Bead Handling Tips

Who spilled the beads? There's no use crying over spilled beads. Instead, try putting a new bag in your vacuum cleaner. Wet the tip of your finger to pick up just a few beads.

They're all wet! A moistened paper towel, wrung out a little, reduces the static electricity that builds up around glass beads. Place the wet towel on your flat container while working.

Mexican jumping beads! If you store your beads in a plastic bag, they will probably try to jump out when you open it up. Blow into the bag lightly and the moisture from your breath will settle the beads enough to pour them out.

Temptation. It is very tempting to loop away without recounting your beads after threading on a very long row. You will only do this once. If you have to rip out a row, first, pull the needle off the thread. Then, use the tip of the needle to gently pull the thread out of the beads.

Organization. Sort beads and place them in small containers with flat, small lipped lids. A muffin tin may also come in handy as a useful organizer.

Seed Bead Needleweaving

The following instructions illustrate the basic technique of bead needleweaving. Aquaint yourself with this technique by experimenting with the instructions and diagrams on the next few pages. Before you know it, you will have discovered the magic of "beauty and the beads."

In these instructions, the vertical rows are numbered from left to right. Row 1 is leftmost for a right-handed person. A left-handed person should start with the highest numbered row and work right to left. The work always proceeds the direction of your dominant hand. The beads of each row are numbered from 1, beginning at the top of each vertical row and increasing to the bottom of the row. The diagrams show a 12-bead row.

Cut a length of thread about 30" long and thread a needle so that a 5" tail remains. A longer thread will tend to tangle, and a shorter thread will necessitate frequent rethreadings.

Slip one bead of any color over the needle, and position it about 3" from the long end of the thread. Loop the thread back through the bead and pull it tightly. The purpose of this "stopper" bead is to keep the design pattern beads from slipping off the needle. It will be removed after a few rows. Secure the stopper bead to a flat or slightly curved surface to stabilize the thread. Some suggestions are a tabletop, the arm of a chair, or a small cushion.

Thread the beads of row 1 from top to bottom; see Diagram B. Skip the last bead threaded, inserting the needle back through all the beads on the thread. The needle should emerge from the top bead of row 1.

Draw a line through the first vertical row of the chart to show that it has been completed.

Thread the beads of row 2, again reading from top to bottom; see Diagram C. Always recount the beads against the pattern to be sure they are in order.

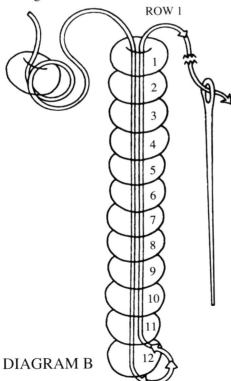

DIAGRAM B

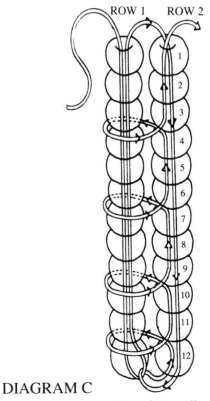

DIAGRAM C

Insert the needle into the loop exposed at the bottom of row 1. Pull the thread gently until the whole second row is taut but not tight and can rest against the first row without much puckering.

Insert the needle into the last bead of row 2 (bead 12) and bring the thread out until it is taut but not tight. Loop the thread around row 1 so that it nestles in the space between beads 12 and 11 of row 2, bringing the needle out in the space between beads 10 and 9 on row 2. Again, bring the thread taut but not tight.

Loop the thread around row 1 so the thread nestles in the space between beads 10 and 9 of row 1. Insert the needle into the next three beads on row 2 (beads 9,8 and 7) and bring the needle out in the space between beads 7 and 6 on row 2.

Tighten the thread again, then loop it around the first row so that it nestles in the space between beads 7 and 6 on row 1. Insert the needle into the next three beads on row 2 (beads 6,5 and 4) and repeat the looping-inserting process until the thread emerges from bead 1 of row 2. After row 2, you may no longer need to stabilize the work. It will get easier and easier to handle as the weaving grows.

All subsequent rows will be worked the same, except that the first loop (nestled between beads 12 and 11 on row 1) will not be made. It is added to the first row to stabilize the work, but is not especially needed in the following rows. The pattern of loops may be worked in any way. If you wish to make a loop between every bead, you may do so, but a three-bead repeat is the most effective for needleweaving. The more frequently you loop, the stiffer the woven piece will be.

ROW 1   ROW 2   ROW 3

AND BEYOND

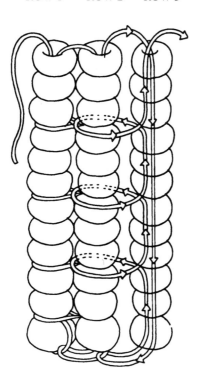

DIAGRAM D

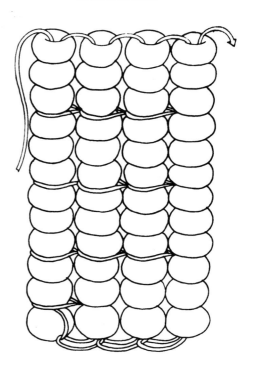

DIAGRAM E

Bugle Bead Needleweaving

Bugle beads are longer than seed beads and therefore the weave goes quickly. This makes bugle beads well suited to any project that might otherwise be tedious and time-consuming. Try using them for purses, belts, bracelets or straps.

Weaving with bugle beads is essentially the same process as weaving with seed beads. The major difference is that in weaving with bugle beads, you should loop between every bead. In weaving with seed beads, you can skip beads and still have a very stable and attractive result. Skipping a loop while weaving bugle beads can mean gaps in the weave and puckering of the finished piece.

It is very important to pay special attention to the tension of your thread while weaving. This is especially important on the first row in which the tone for the entire piece will be established.

Because the holes in bugle beads can be quite small, it is probably a good idea to start with a tiny needle.

Inspect the bugles to see if any are broken or obviously different in length. Try to use beads which are similar in length, or there will be some puckering.

Place a stopper bead on the end of your 30" thread. Thread all beads of the first vertical row. Skip the last bead and run the needle back through all the remaining beads on the thread; see Diagram F. Be especially careful to keep the tension of the thread loose so the bottom bead does not twist.

Thread all beads of row 2. Insert the needle into the bottom bead on row 1 and pull the thread all the way through. Then, insert the needle into the second-to-bottom bead of row 2 and pull the thread all the way through. Loop around row 1 so the loop nestles in the space between beads. Insert the needle in the next bugle bead on row 2 and repeat the looping process until the needle emerges from the top bugle of row 2; see Diagram G.

Thread all bugles of row 3. Run the needle through the small piece of thread that connects the bottom bugles of rows 1 and 2. Insert the needle back into the bottom bead of row 3. Continue looping as in the previous rows until the thread emerges from the top of row 3; see Diagram H. All subsequent rows will be connected at the bottom bead in this manner.

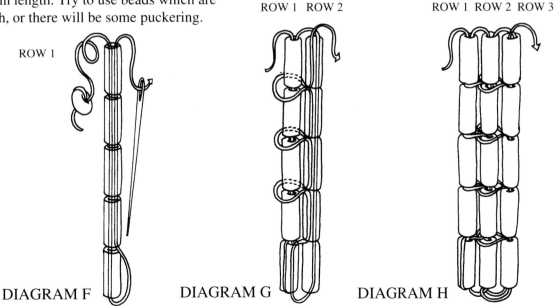

ROW 1

ROW 1 ROW 2

ROW 1 ROW 2 ROW 3

DIAGRAM F　　**DIAGRAM G**　　**DIAGRAM H**

Shaping Flat Weaves

You can add interest to the shape of woven beadwork by increasing or decreasing beads along the bottom edge of the weave. The following diagrams show the looping pattern for one-and two-bead increases and decreases.

Increasing or decreasing at the top edge of a woven piece is quite difficult and should be avoided because the resulting weave is messy-looking in comparison with the rest of the piece. If you work a piece that requires an uneven top edge, you should weave the bottom half of the piece first, then invert the partially completed weave and weave the remainder in reverse. For an example of this, see "Scenes of the Sahara" on page 55.

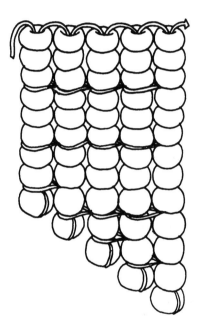

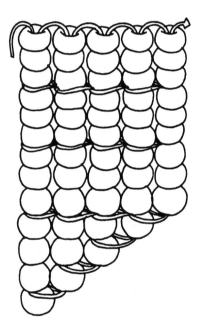

DIAGRAM I

DIAGRAM J

This shows the basic pattern of loops when adding one bead to the length of a looped row. Note that the three-bead loop pattern is resumed in each row as soon as possible. Hangers may be added on increased rows.

This shows the basic pattern of loops for decreasing one bead at the bottom of a row. Be careful not to pull the thread too tightly, especially near the bottom bead.

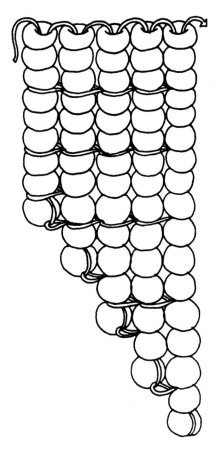

DIAGRAM K

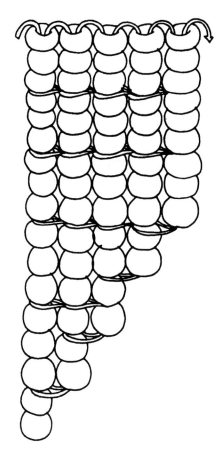

DIAGRAM L

This shows the basic pattern of loops when adding two beads to the length of a looped row. Again, note that the three-bead looping pattern is resumed as soon as possible.

This shows the basic pattern of loops when decreasing two beads at the bottom of each row. Again, be careful to keep the thread tension taut but light.

Joining

When weaving a particularly large piece of beadwork, such as might be used in a purse or makeup case, it is easier to work small pieces and join them together; see Diagram M. It is a good idea to use a very small needle for this procedure because the buildup of thread inside the bead holes can make it difficult to get a larger needle through. If you simply can not get the needle through, skip the clogged bead and go on to the next row. It will not be noticeable in the finished piece.

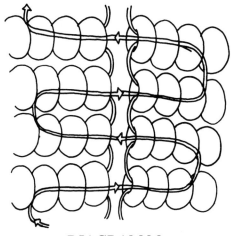

DIAGRAM M

Hangers & Fringes

When designs with hangers or fringes are patterned, there is a separation between the sections that show the foundation pattern (which is looped together) and the hangers (which are not looped). Each will be clearly marked as being either "foundation" or "hangers".

When forming hangers, the tension of the thread is important. Try to leave enough slack so that the hangers move freely, but not so much that there is a lot of visible thread. Part of the beauty of hangers and fringes is their motion. If that motion is impeded by excessive thread tension, there will be something missing from the overall design.

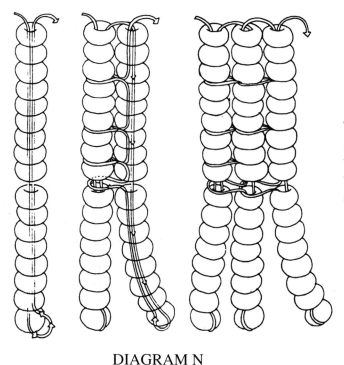

DIAGRAM N

The three-bead end (also know as a "picot") is worked by skipping the last three beads and running the needle back through the remaining bead on the hanger. Don't pull it too tightly, and try to settle the beads evenly at the end; see Diagram O. Try using one color for the last four beads. It will form a diamond and give an interesting dimension to the design.

DIAGRAM O

The simple one-bead end finish is worked by skipping the last bead and running the needle back through the remaining beads on the hanger. Be sure to nestle the bead sideways for a neat appearance; see Diagram P.

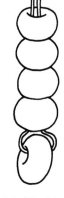

DIAGRAM P

Finishing Touches

Finishing a Tube

Finishing a tube is simply a matter of securing the woven beadwork neatly around the foundation material of your choice. Ordinary clothesline is a nice foundation for a three-dimensional tube.

After all the weaving is completed, trim any excess threads that occur in the body of the weave. If there is a long piece of thread left at the end of the weave, use this to begin sewing the long edges together. Otherwise, bury a new thread within the weave at one end.

Cut a length of clothesline that will be at least 1" longer than the planned length of the tube. Wrap the woven length around the clothesline at the threaded end and weave the edges together. Line up the beads on one edge of the strip to the beads in the same row on the other edge of the strip; see Diagram Q.

Continue weaving back and forth until the entire length has been joined together. Trim the ends of the clothesline very closely to the end of the weave. It may be necessary to use a very small needle.

Finish the ends with seed beads that coordinate or complement the design of the piece you are finishing. Have the thread emerge from one of the beads on the outermost row of the weave on either end. Work rounds of beads according to the following instructions and Diagram R.

Round 1. Work two beads into each group of three beads around the end. This reduces the number of beads on the round from 18 to 12.

Round 2. Work one bead into each group of two beads in the round of 12 beads. This reduces the number of beads from 12 to six.

Round 3. Run the thread through the remaining six beads and tighten it just so the gap closes. Do not pull it too tightly or the end will pucker. Bury the remaining thread in the weave (not the clothesline) and trim it.

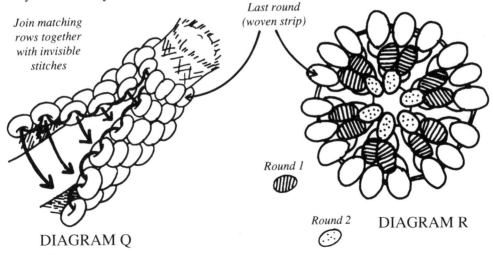

Join matching rows together with invisible stitches

DIAGRAM Q

Last round (woven strip)

Round 1

Round 2　DIAGRAM R

Attaching Backing

To finish the back of woven projects, you will need scissors, lightweight cardboard (such as a piece of cereal box), common pins, needle and thread, fabric that coordinates with beaded piece and tacky glue.

1. Lay the finished beadwork face down on the cardboard. Insert pins into the cardboard at the corners of the woven piece to mark the shape; see Diagram S.

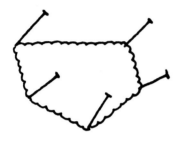

DIAGRAM S

2. Connect the dots, then cut the cardboard about ⅛ " smaller all around than the marked shape; see Diagram T.

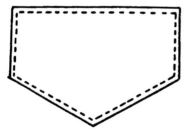

DIAGRAM T

3. Using the cut cardboard as a guide, cut a piece of fabric with a margin of about ½" all around. Notch fabric at all corners; see Diagram U.

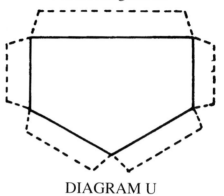

DIAGRAM U

4. Center the cut cardboard shape on the fabric. Put several small dots of glue on the back of the fabric. Fold the edges of the fabric over the cardboard and glue the edges lightly; see Diagram V.

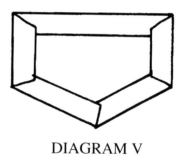

DIAGRAM V

5. Position the fabric-covered cardboard on the back of the beadwork. Secure it to the beadwork with small invisible stitches; see Diagram W. When attaching a pinback or barrette, sew right through the cardboard, if possible.

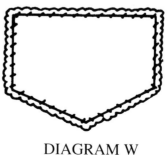

DIAGRAM W

SOUTHWEST PIN & EARRINGS

SOUTHWEST PIN & EARRINGS

Materials for pin

11/0 seed beads:
- 835 opaque lustered cream
- 366 opaque red
- 92 opaque brown
- 97 metallic silver
- 188 opaque black

33 opaque lustered cream 6/0 seed beads
3" x 4" fabric piece for backing
3" x 4" lightweight cardboard piece
1½" pinback

Materials for earrings

11/0 seed beads:
- 90 opaque black
- 144 opaque red
- 36 opaque brown
- 334 opaque lustered cream
- 108 metallic silver

18 opaque lustered cream 6/0 seed beads
4" clothesline length
One pair of silver-finish earwires

Directions:

See Accessorize in Pastels pin
and earrings on pages 28 and 29.

SYMBOL GUIDE

- ⬭ opaque lustered cream 11/0
- ◉ metallic silver 11/0
- ⬌ opaque red 11/0
- ⬔ opaque brown 11/0
- ⬕ opaque black 11/0
- ⬯ opaque lustered cream 6/0

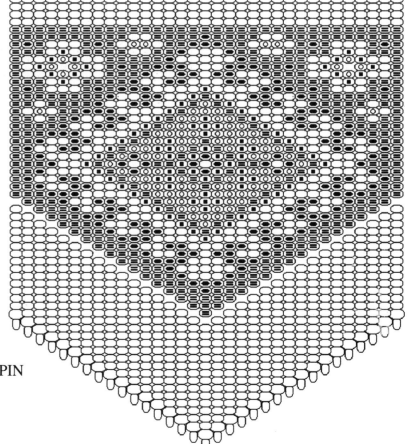

**SOUTHWEST PIN
PATTERN**

SOUTHWEST EARRING PATTERN

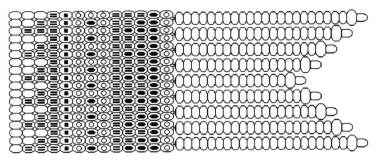

FOUNDATION   FRINGES

MAGIC CARPET PIN PATTERN

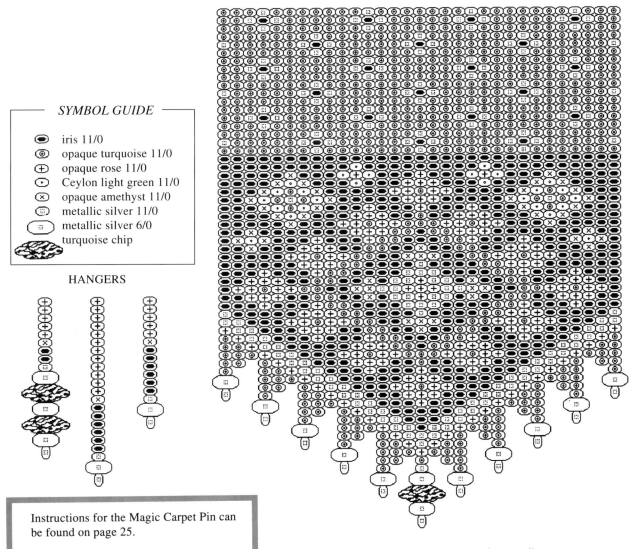

SYMBOL GUIDE

- ◉ iris 11/0
- ◎ opaque turquoise 11/0
- ⊕ opaque rose 11/0
- ⊙ Ceylon light green 11/0
- ⊗ opaque amethyst 11/0
- ⊞ metallic silver 11/0
- ⬭ metallic silver 6/0
- ▨ turquoise chip

HANGERS

Instructions for the Magic Carpet Pin can be found on page 25.

ART DECO PIN

Materials

11/0 seed beads:
  496 silver-lined crystal
  112 color-lined rose
  106 color-lined iris
  256 opaque black
119 silver-lined aqua #2 bugle beads

Two clear pink 6mm glass beads
Seven black 4mm English cut beads
3" x 4" fabric piece for backing
3" x 4" lightweight cardboard piece
1½" pinback

Directions

1. Weave design piece according to Art Deco Pin pattern.

2. Sew one clear pink 6mm glass bead to top center over black patch, weaving thread into design and then burying thread after sewing bead. Bring thread ends to back of design.

3. Attach backing fabric and lightweight cardboard to foundation.

4. Sew pinback.

Hint: When trimming the mounting cardboard for this design, do not try to match the shape of the foundation pattern exactly. Cut a simple v-shape for the bottom edge, being sure it does not show below the bottom edge of the foundation.

ART DECO PIN PATTERN

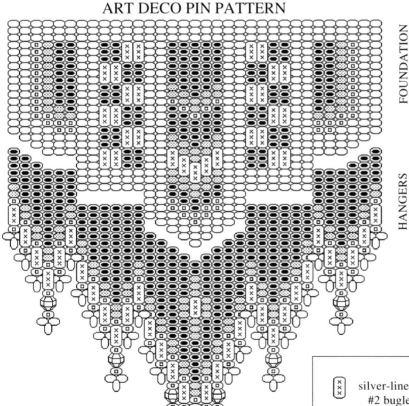

FOUNDATION

HANGERS

SYMBOL GUIDE

silver-lined aqua 11/0 #2 bugle beads	black 4mm English cut beads
clear pink 6mm glass beads	color-lined iris 11/0
silver-lined crystal 11/0	color-lined rose 11/0
3-bead end	black 4mm English cut beads

ART DECO PIN

MAGIC CARPET PIN

MAGIC CARPET PIN

Materials

11/0 seed beads:
- 633 opaque turquoise
- 478 iris
- 184 metallic silver
- 225 opaque rose
- 62 opaque amethyst
- 26 Ceylon light green

21 metallic silver 6/0 seed beads
Five turquoise chips
5" clothesline length
1½" pinback

Directions

1. Weave design piece according to **Magic Carpet Pin** pattern on page 21.

2. Cut clothesline to ¼" longer than top edge of woven beadwork. Wrap all around with masking tape to stiffen.

3. Wrap top 18 rows of woven piece around clothesline and stitch tube top edge to the 18th horizontal row with small invisible stitches.

4. Close tube top ends using opaque turquoise 11/0 seed beads; see section on "Finishing a Tube" on page 17.

5. Bring a thread out at end of tube and add hangers on both sides according to pattern.

6. Sew pinback to back of tube top.

Materials for barrette

11/0 seed beads:
- 146 metallic gold
- 260 Ceylon pink
- 52 Ceylon turquoise
- 52 Ceylon purple
- 52 Ceylon medium blue
- 53 Ceylon light green

1" x 4" fabric piece for backing
1" x 4" lightweight cardboard piece
3" barrette blank

Directions

1. Weave entire piece according to barrette pattern.

2. Apply backing fabric and lightweight cardboard.

3. Stitch finished piece onto barrette blank.

BARRETTE PATTERN

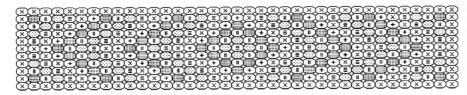

SYMBOL GUIDE

- Ceylon turquoise 11/0
- Ceylon purple 11/0
- metallic gold 11/0
- Ceylon medium blue 11/0
- Ceylon pink 11/0
- Ceylon light green 11/0

Materials for earrings

11/0 seed beads:
- 54 dark iris
- 54 Ceylon turquoise
- 27 Ceylon purple
- 52 Ceylon pink
- 342 metallic gold
- 54 Ceylon medium blue
- 54 Ceylon light green

4" clothesline length
One pair of gold-finished earwires

Directions

1. Weave foundation according to earring pattern.

2. Turn both pieces sideways and make fringes.

3. Wrap each stitched piece around clothesline and finish end; see section on "Finishing a Tube" on page 17.

4. Sew earwires to both earrings.

EARRING PATTERN

FOUNDATION   FRINGES

Materials for necklace

11/0 seed beads:
- 141 dark iris
- 360 metallic gold
- 72 Ceylon turquoise
- 72 Ceylon purple
- 235 Ceylon pink
- 72 Ceylon medium blue
- 72 Ceylon light green

8" clothesline length
Two 18" pieces of rattail cord in a coordinating color

Directions

1. Weave entire piece according to pattern on page 29 .

2. Following directions for earrings, wrap woven piece around clothesline and finish ends using metallic gold beads.

3. Add small bead loops at both ends.

4. From rattail lengths, make necklace ends as shown; see Diagram.

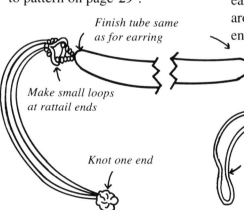

Finish tube same as for earring

Make small loops at rattail ends

Knot one end

Stitch one end together, forming loop

DIAGRAM

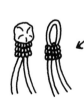

Wrap 3 loops of gold beads around both ends

NECKLACE PATTERN

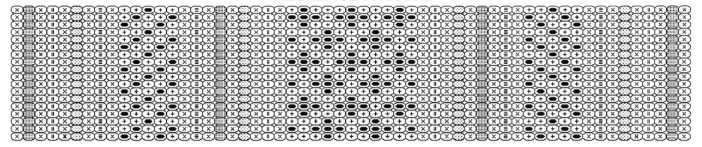

Materials for pin

11/0 seed beads:
  68 dark iris
  105 Ceylon turquoise
  77 Ceylon purple
  314 metallic gold
  113 Ceylon light blue
  284 Ceylon pink
  131 Ceylon light green

2" x 4" fabric piece for backing
2" x 4" lightweight cardboard piece
1½" pinback

Directions

1. Weave entire piece according to pattern.

2. Attach backing fabric and lightweight cardboard to foundation.

3. Attach pinback.

SYMBOL GUIDE

- ◕ dark iris 11/0
- ◌ Ceylon turquoise 11/0
- ◓ Ceylon purple 11/0
- ⊗ metallic gold 11/0
- ⊕ Ceylon medium blue 11/0
- ⊕ Ceylon pink 11/0
- ⊟ Ceylon light green 11/0
- ⊗ 3-bead end

PIN PATTERN

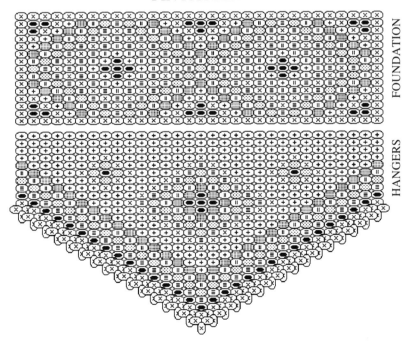

FOUNDATION

HANGERS

TOPAZ EARRINGS

TOPAZ EARRINGS

Materials

11/0 seed beads:
   730 metallic gold
   96 metallic copper
   586 transparent iris dark amber

18 satin caramel #3 bugle beads
18 AB finished light amber 4mm crystals
One pair of gold-finished earwires
4" clothesline length

Directions

1. Weave foundation piece according to Topaz Earring pattern.

2. Make fringes according to pattern, attaching at edge of foundation.

3. Wrap foundation around clothesline and weave edges together; see section on "Joining" on page 15.

4. Cap tube end using transparent dark amber iris; see section on "Finishing a Tube" on page 17.

5. Trim clothesline at bottom edge of foundation.

6. Sew earwires to top circle of six beads; do not sew to clothes-line.

SYMBOL GUIDE

◎ metallic gold 11/0
○ metallic copper 11/0
● transparent iris
   dark amber 11/0
▯ satin carmel
   #3 bugle bead
⬡ AB finished light
   amber 4mm crystal
⚬ 3-bead end (copper)

TOPAZ EARRING PATTERN

FOUNDATION   FRINGES

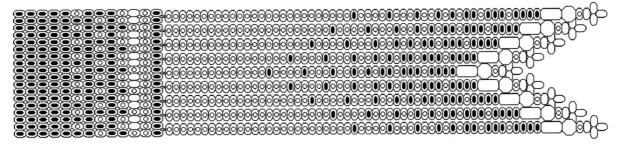

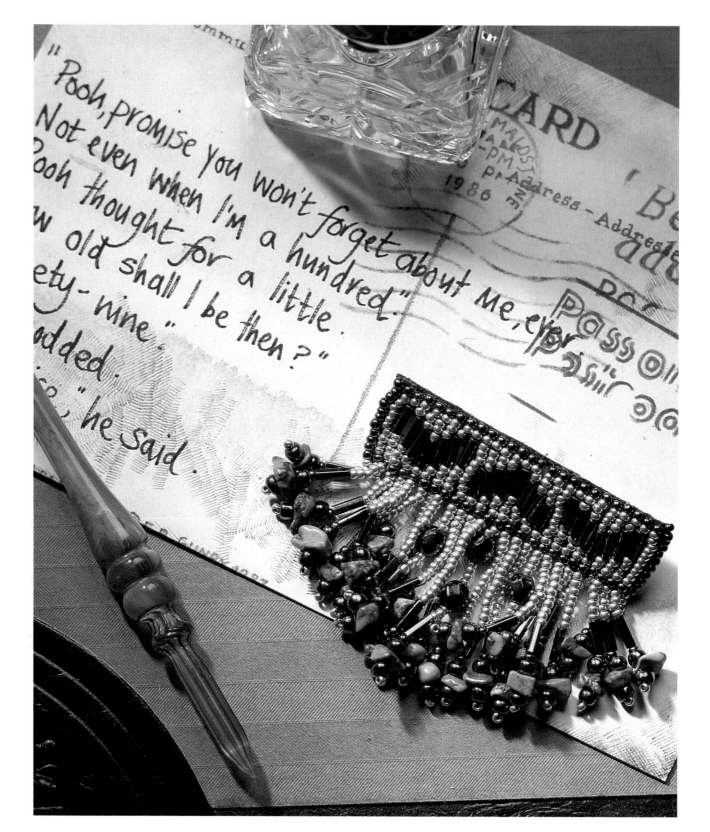

TURQUOISE CHEVRON PIN

TURQUOISE CHEVRON PIN

Materials

27 turquoise chips
48 iris purple #3 bugle beads
Four iris purple 6mm crystals
54 iris purple 6/0 seed beads
126 iris purple 11/0 seed beads

382 metallic gold 11/0 seed beads
1" x 3" fabric piece for backing
1" x 3" lightweight cardboard piece
1½" pinback

Directions

1. Weave the entire piece according to Turquoise Chevron Pin pattern.

2. Finish back with fabric and lightweight cardboard.

3. Sew pinback.

Hint: Try to use bugles that are close in size, especially in the foundation pattern. Sort through your bugle beads and discard any that are obviously larger or smaller. Try to choose turquoise chips of similar size, avoiding those that are very narrow or very long. They should be "chunky" in shape.

TURQUOISE CHEVRON PIN PATTERN

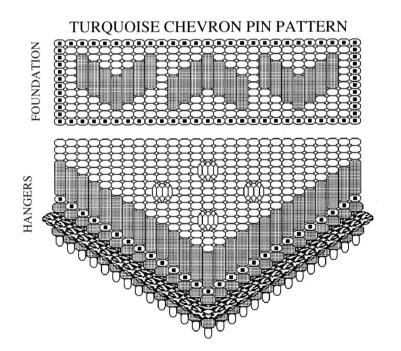

FOUNDATION

HANGERS

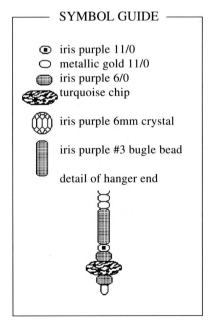

SYMBOL GUIDE

- ⊙ iris purple 11/0
- ○ metallic gold 11/0
- ▦ iris purple 6/0
- turquoise chip
- iris purple 6mm crystal
- iris purple #3 bugle bead

detail of hanger end

VICTORIAN DROP PIN

VICTORIAN DROP PIN

Materials

11/0 seed beads:
- 400 metallic gold
- 362 iris green
- 72 opaque lustered cream
- 97 color-lined light green
- 82 opaque medium green
- 40 color-lined rose
- 99 opaque light rose
- 59 Ceylon lavender
- 76 color-lined purple

33 iris green 8/0 seed beads
33 iris aqua 12mm bugle beads
Two clear pink 8mm seed beads
One AB finished Austrian 12mm crystal
3" x 4" fabric piece for backing
3" x 4" lightweight cardboard piece
1½" pinback

Directions

1. Weave design according to Victorian Drop Pin pattern.

2. Attach fabric and lightweight cardboard to foundation.

3. Sew pinback.

SYMBOL GUIDE

- ⬭ clear pink 8mm bead
- ⊙ iris green 8/0
- ⊗ metallic gold 11/0
- ⬬ iris green 11/0
- ⬓ opaque medium green 11/0
- ⬭ opaque lustered cream 11/0
- ⬮ Ceylon lavender 11/0
- ⬤ color-lined purple 11/0
- ◎ opaque light rose 11/0
- ◉ color-lined rose 11/0
- ◔ color-lined light green 11/0
- 3-bead end
- AB finished Austrian 12mm crystal
- iris aqua 12mm bugle bead

VICTORIAN DROP PIN PATTERN

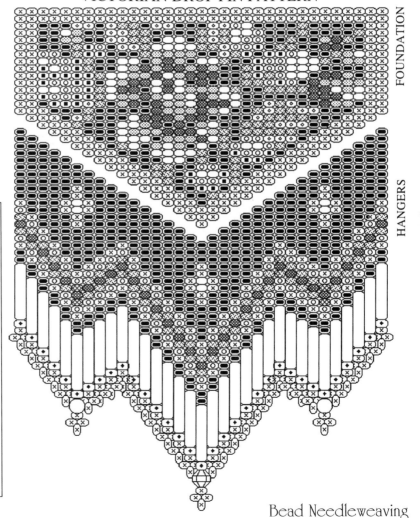

FOUNDATION

HANGERS

きっとまだわたしの知らない

どこかの林の中に、

ある季節だけこんな花が

少しずつ咲いているのではないかしら

思ってつくりました。

林の奥は日の光も

よく届けられないで

花たちは少し小さめで

青みを持たせて

もらうのかもしれません。P.1

PAGODA PIN

PAGODA PIN

Materials

10/0 seed beads:
   182 opaque dark blue
   613 lustered ivory
   298 opaque medium blue
   214 opaque light blue
   206 metallic silver

Three AB firepolished light sapphire 8mm
   crystals
One lapis chip
3" x 4" fabric piece for backing
3" x 4" lightweight cardboard piece
1½" pinback

Directions

1. Weave entire piece according to Pagoda Pin pattern.

2. Apply backing fabric and lightweight cardboard to foundation.

3. Sew pinback.

PAGODA PIN PATTERN

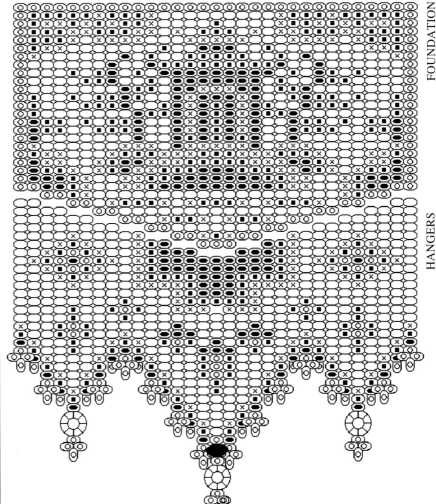

FOUNDATION

HANGERS

SYMBOL GUIDE

- AB firepolished light sapphire 8mm crystal
- opaque dark blue 10/0
- lustered ivory 10/0
- opaque medium blue 10/0
- opaque light blue 10/0
- metallic silver 10/0
- lapis chip
- 3-bead end

NEON BLUE BARRETTE

NEON BLUE BARRETTE

Materials

11/0 seed beads:
  623 Ceylon pale lavender
  305 silver-lined dark blue
  262 metallic pink
  226 transparent rainbow light
      sapphire

1" x 4" fabric piece for backing
1" x 4" lightweight cardboard piece
3" barrette blank

Directions

1. Weave entire piece according to Neon Blue Barrette pattern.

2. Attach backing fabric and lightweight cardboard to foundation.

3. Sew barrette blank.

NEON BLUE BARRETTE PATTERN

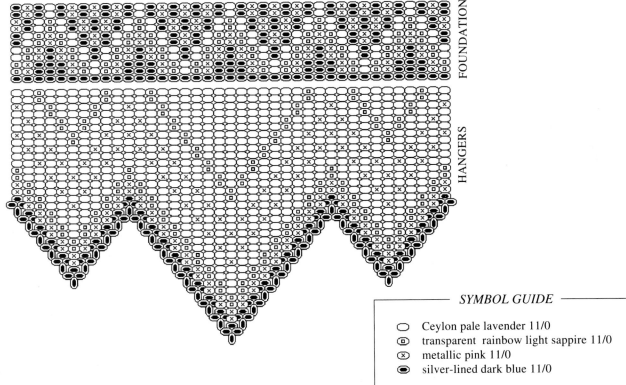

SYMBOL GUIDE

◯ Ceylon pale lavender 11/0
◉ transparent rainbow light sappire 11/0
⊗ metallic pink 11/0
⬤ silver-lined dark blue 11/0

FLAPPER NECKLACE

FLAPPER NECKLACE

Materials

1oz. cream 11/0 seed beads
1oz. silver-lined purple 11/0 seed beads

15" clothesline length
One clasp set

Directions

1. Weave two tube pieces according to pattern below.

2. Join each piece together around clothesline; see section on "Joining" on page 15.

3. Trim clothesline to same length as woven tube.

4. Make two fringe sections according to pattern below. Attach ends to inside ends of both tubes.

5. Make chains according to pattern on page 42, attaching to outside edges of both tubes.

6. Join together ends of chains and sew clasp.

7. At fringe ends, sew tubes together with a few invisible stitches. Pull together two fringe strands from each side; knot.

SYMBOL GUIDE

○   cream 11/0 seed bead
◉   silver-lined purple 11/0 seed bead

TUBE PATTERN

ATTACH CHAINS   ATTACH FRINGE

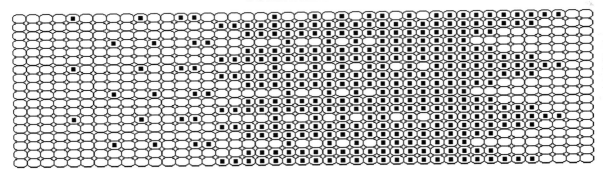

FRINGE PATTERN

ATTACH TO TUBE

=30 cream plus=
=33 cream plus=
=36 cream plus=
=39 cream plus=
=42 cream plus=
=45 cream plus=
=48 cream plus=
=51 cream plus=
=54 cream plus=

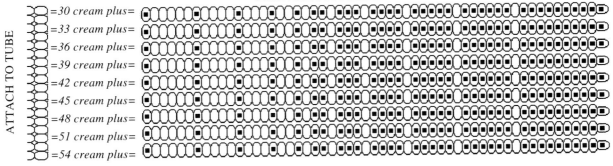

CHAIN PATTERN

ATTACH CLASP

*50 SILVER-LINED
PURPLE 11/0 PLUS*

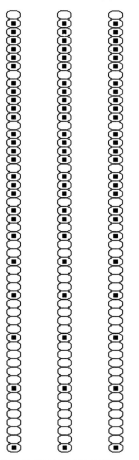

25 CREAM 11/0 PLUS

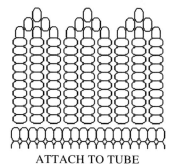

ATTACH TO TUBE

SIDE PANEL PATTERN

ORIENTAL CARPET PURSE

ATTACH TO CENTER PANEL

Instructions for the Oriental Carpet Purse can be found on page 44.

ORIENTAL CARPET PURSE

Materials

11/0 seed beads:
   422 Ceylon cream
   1360 Ceylon silver
   1100 Ceylon copper
   1022 Ceylon turquoise
   915 iris green
   422 Ceylon light blue

⅜ yard of turquoise satin
Two 1 yard lengths of turquoise rattail
   cording

Directions

1. Weave one center panel and two side panels according to Oriental Carpet Purse pattern on pages 42 and 45.

2. Join panels together matching pattern; see section on "Joining" on page 15.

3. To cut fabric, measure the width of beaded piece adding 1". Measure the length of the beaded piece, double and add 2"; see Diagram A.

WIDTH + 1"

TWO TIMES LENGTH + 2"

DIAGRAM A

4. Fold fabric in half with short ends aligned. Sew sides together with a ½" seam allowance, stopping 1" from open top; see Diagram B.

DIAGRAM B

5. Clip bottom corners on each side and press seams back against lining; see Diagram C.

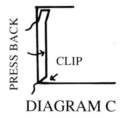

PRESS BACK

CLIP

DIAGRAM C

6. Topstitch folded 1" unsewn seam at top of opening; see Diagram D. Repeat on other side seam.

DIAGRAM D

7. Double fold top, open edges under ½"; press. Handstitch fold to lining back along bottom of fold; see Diagram E.

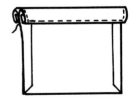

DIAGRAM E

8. Feed one length of rattail cording through one folded top seam, looping and feeding length back through seam; see Diagram F. Repeat with remaining length and folded seam.

DIAGRAM F

9. Knot ends of rattail length together at each side; see Diagram G.

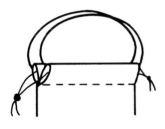

DIAGRAM G

10. Position beaded piece on one side of lining with edges aligned. Slipstitch together.

SYMBOL GUIDE

⬭	Ceylon cream 11/0
⊕	Ceylon silver 11/0
⊜	Ceylon copper 11/0
◎	Ceylon turquoise 11/0
⬤	iris green 11/0
⊟	Ceylon light blue 11/0

SIDE PANEL PATTERN
ON PAGE 42

CENTER PANEL PATTERN

ATTACH SIDE PANEL HERE

ATTACH SIDE PANEL HERE

 MEDICINE POUCH NECKLACE

MEDICINE POUCH NECKLACE

Materials	
11/0 seed beads:	One iris firepolished 6mm crystal
470 iris purple	1 yard of aqua rattail cording
413 opaque purple	
311 opaque aqua	
413 opaque pink	
686 opaque light blue	

Directions

1. Weave pouch piece according to pattern on page 48 .

2. Fold squared edge up toward chevron, eight rows below the beginning of diagonal edge. Stitch sides together to form small pouch.

3. Make fringes according to pattern below, attaching at folded edge of pouch piece. Bury thread within weave, working fringe rows all across folded bottom according to pattern.

4. Using 20 iris purple beads, make small loop at point of chevron flap. Checking flap for proper placement, sew 6mm crystal to front of pouch so loop slips over like a buttonhole.

5. Center and sew pouch piece to rattail cording. Run rattail under fold-line of flap, attaching inside flap with invisible stitches.

FRINGE PATTERN

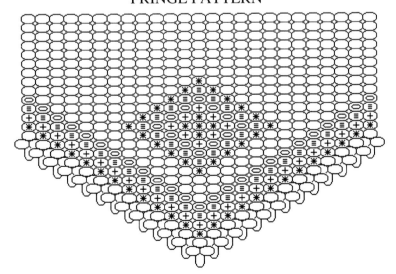

SYMBOL GUIDE	
✳	iris purple 11/0
⊕	opaque purple 11/0
⊟	opaque aqua 11/0
⬭	opaque pink 11/0
⬭	opaque light blue 11/0

POUCH PATTERN

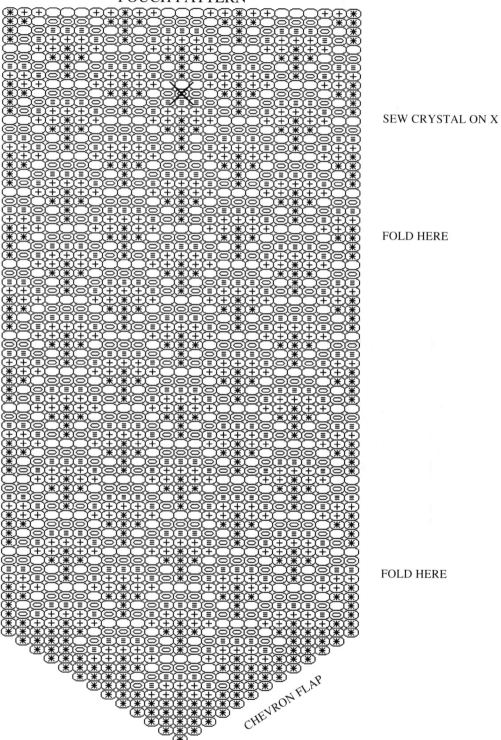

SEW CRYSTAL ON X

FOLD HERE

FOLD HERE

CHEVRON FLAP

48   Bead Needleweaving

ATTACH BEAD LOOP HERE

IRIS SPHERE EARRINGS

Materials

450 iris green 11/0 seed beads
Four metallic gold 6/0 seed beads

Two 1" Styrofoam balls
One pair of gold-finished earwires

Directions

Round 1. Thread five beads and make a loop by passing needle through all five; see Diagram A. Pull gently until thread is taut.

5 beads in a loop
DIAGRAM A

Round 2. Work two beads in each bead on loop (ten beads); see Diagram B.

2 beads in each 1 bead
DIAGRAM B

Round 3. Work two beads in each bead on the round (20 beads); see Diagram C.

2 beads in 2 beads
DIAGRAM C

Round 4. Work two beads in first two beads, two beads in next two beads and two beads in next one bead. Repeat (24 beads).

Round 5. Work two beads in first two beads, two beads in next two beads and three beads in next two beads; see Diagram D. Repeat (28 beads).

3 beads in 2 beads
DIAGRAM D

Round 6. Work two beads in first two beads, two beads in next two beads and two beads in next one bead. Repeat (32 beads).

Round 7. Work two beads in first two beads, two beads in next two beads, two beads in next two beads and three beads in next two beads. Repeat (36 beads).

Round 8. Work two beads in first two beads, two beads in next two beads, two beads in next two beads and two beads in next one bead. Repeat (40 beads).

Round 9. Work two beads in each two beads.

Round 10. Repeat Round 9.

Round 11. Work two beads in first two beads, two beads in next two beads, two beads in next two beads and two beads in next three beads; see Diagram E. Repeat (32 beads). Slip Styrofoam ball in woven cup.

Round 12. Work two beads in first two beads, two beads in next two beads, two beads in next two beads and two beads in next three beads; see Diagram E. Repeat (32 beads).

Round 13. Work two beads in first two beads, two beads in next two beads, two beads in next two beads and one bead in next two beads; see Diagram F. Repeat (28 beads).

Round 14. Work two beads in first two beads, two beads in next two beads and two beads in next three beads. Repeat (24 beads).

Round 15. Work two beads in first two beads, two beads in next two beads and two beads in next three beads. Repeat (24 beads).

Round 16. Work one bead in each two beads (ten beads).

Round 17. Work one bead in each two beads (five beads).

Finishing

1. Weave thread into bottom of sphere and stitch one metallic gold 6/0 seed bead anchored by one iris green 11/0 seed bead. Repeat at top and bottom of both spheres, burying thread end into weave and clipping close afterward.

2. Sew earwires to top of each sphere.

2 beads in 3 beads
DIAGRAM E

1 bead in 2 beads
DIAGRAM F

 RIBBON PIN

RIBBON PIN

Materials

11/0 seed beads:
- 495 metallic gold
- 161 opaque lustered cream
- 44 metallic pink
- Nine metallic red
- 24 metallic dark green
- 28 metallic light green

8" length of ⅜" purple ribbon
1" x 3" fabric piece for backing
1" x 3" lightweight cardboard piece
1½" pinback

Directions

1. Weave foundation and fringes according to Ribbon Pin pattern.

2. Sew edging following thread path on pattern.

3. Apply backing fabric and lightweight cardboard to foundation.

4. Gather fringes together and tie ribbon bow about ¾" below foundation of pin.

5. Sew pinback.

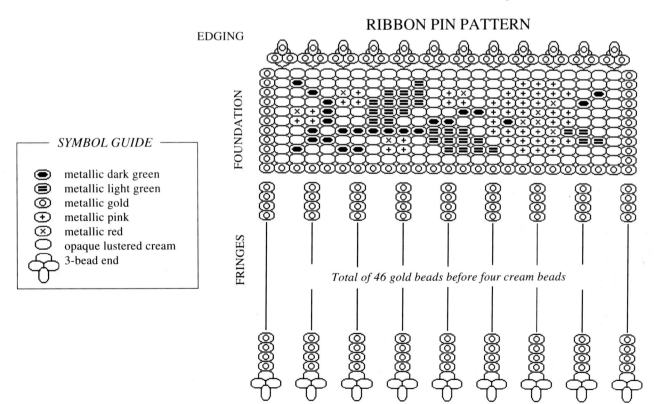

RIBBON PIN PATTERN

EDGING

FOUNDATION

FRINGES

Total of 46 gold beads before four cream beads

SYMBOL GUIDE

- metallic dark green
- metallic light green
- metallic gold
- metallic pink
- metallic red
- opaque lustered cream
- 3-bead end

JUNE

SUN   MON   TUES   WED   THURS   FRI   SAT

SCENES of the SAHARA

Materials

11/0 seed beads:
   2 oz. metallic gold
   38 Ceylon yellow
   13 opaque lustered white
   114 Ceylon turquoise
   70 Ceylon medium purple
   74 opaque lustered tangerine
   128 lustered red
   579 iris opaque green
   170 transparent color-lined iris
   36 Ceylon light blue
   24 Ceylon pale pink

23" clothesline length
Hook-and-eye set for closure

Directions

1. Weave design piece according to Sahara pattern on page 56; set aside.

2. Weave necklace following small section of pattern below; repeat until entire piece measures 21" long.

3. Wrap necklace piece around clothesline and weave edges together; see section on "Joining" on page 15.

4. Finish tube ends using metallic gold; see section on "Finishing A Tube" on page 17.

5. Center and sew design piece on necklace tube using small invisible stitches. Run thread up through center design weave and into weave of tube, repeating until entire piece is secure.

6. Sew hook-and-eye set to tube ends.

SYMBOL GUIDE

⊙   Ceylon yellow 11/0
◯   opaque lustered white 11/0
⬢   Ceylon turquoise 11/0
⬤   Ceylon medium purple 11/0
⊜   opaque lustered tangerine 11/0
⊕   lustered red 11/0
⬤   iris opaque green 11/0
⊜   transparent color-lined iris 11/0
⊗   metallic gold 11/0
Ⓘ   Ceylon light blue 11/0
⊕   Ceylon pale pink 11/0

NECKLACE PATTERN

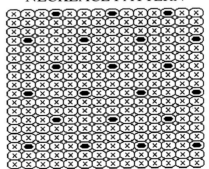

SAHARA PATTERN

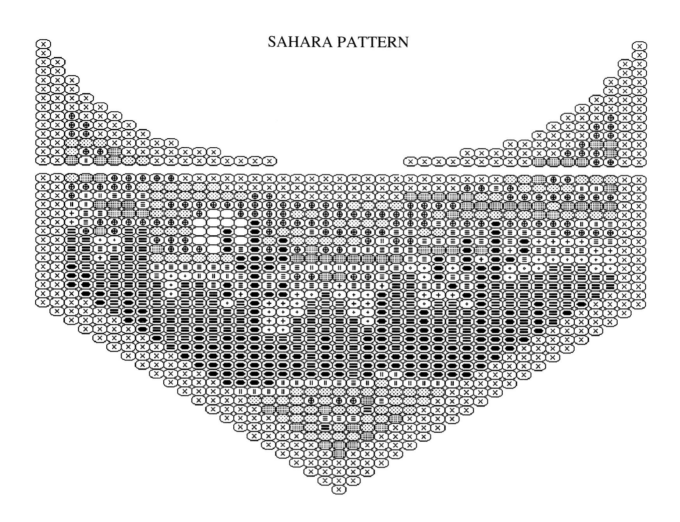

Work the lower, chevron-shaped section first. Then, invert the pattern and work the upper corners as if they were at the bottom edge of the design. Pay special attention to the bead alignment.

NAVAJO ARTIFACTS

Materials for barrette

11/0 seed beads:
- 78 opaque black
- 70 metallic copper
- 71 Ceylon turquoise
- 202 metallic silver

1" x 5" fabric piece for backing
1" x 5" lightweight cardboard piece
3" barrette blank

Materials for earrings

11/0 seed beads:
- 108 opaque black
- 126 metallic copper
- 180 Ceylon turquoise
- 334 metallic silver
- 90 Ceylon cream

4" clothesline length
One pair of silver-finish earwires

Materials for necklace

11/0 seed beads:
- 195 opaque black
- 266 metallic copper
- 164 Ceylon turquoise
- 299 metallic silver
- 138 Ceylon cream

8" clothesline length
Two 20" black rattail cording lengths

Materials for pin

11/0 seed beads:
- 262 opaque black
- 92 metallic copper
- 227 Ceylon turquoise
- 120 metallic silver
- 56 Ceylon cream

3" x 3" fabric piece for backing
3" x 3" lightweight cardboard piece
1½" pinback

Directions

See Accessorize in Pastels barrette, earrings, necklace and pin on pages 27, 28 and 29.

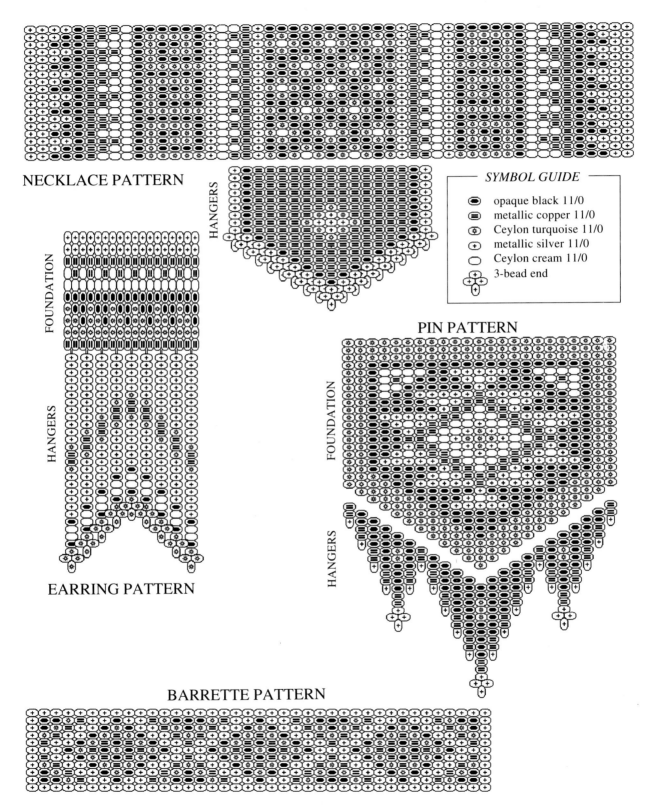

NECKLACE PATTERN

HANGERS

FOUNDATION

HANGERS

EARRING PATTERN

SYMBOL GUIDE

- opaque black 11/0
- metallic copper 11/0
- Ceylon turquoise 11/0
- metallic silver 11/0
- Ceylon cream 11/0
- 3-bead end

PIN PATTERN

FOUNDATION

HANGERS

BARRETTE PATTERN

BARGELLO PIN

BARGELLO PIN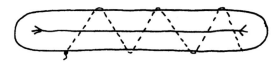

Materials

#2 bugle beads:
- 68 silver-lined crystal
- 49 silver-lined pink
- 46 silver-lined light aqua
- 38 silver-lined sapphire
- 30 iris

Eight clear pink 8mm glass beads
65 silver-lined crystal 10/0 seed beads

Ten AB finished transparent sapphire 6/0 seed beads
One frosted amethyst 10mm donut-shaped rondelle
6" clothesline length
10 yards of metallic silver fiber (similar in weight to embroidery floss)
1½" pinback

Directions

1. Trim raw ends of clothesline. Wrap ordinary sewing thread around each end to prevent ravelling; see Diagram A.

DIAGRAM A

2. Form circle with trimmed clothesline. Join ends together, stitching to secure; see Diagram B.

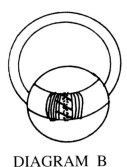

DIAGRAM B

3. Wrap entire circle using metallic silver fiber; see Diagram C.

Lay a loop over the clothesline.

Wrap silver thread around loop.

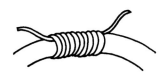

When little thread remains, tuck free end into loop. Pull thread from both ends until loop disappears into wrap.

DIAGRAM C

4. Form the wrapped circle into a long bar. Secure with thread; see Diagram D.

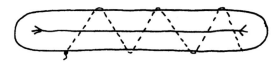

Sew through the wrapped circle to flatten it into an elongated bar.

DIAGRAM D

5. Weave design piece according to Bargello Pin pattern on page 62.

6. Center and sew hanging piece to bar; see Diagram E on page 62.

7. Sew decorative beads on bar, adjusting beads to fill space neatly; see Bar pattern on page 62.

8. Sew pinback to center back of bar.

DIAGRAM E

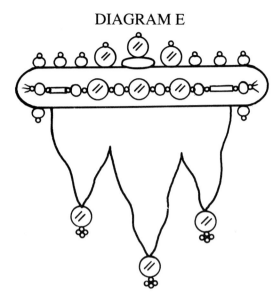

This section is woven separately and then attached to the silver-wrapped bar with small stitches using ordinary sewing thread. Run the needle through the finished weave to secure the thread, then sew right through the bar to attach securely.

BAR PATTERN

SYMBOL GUIDE

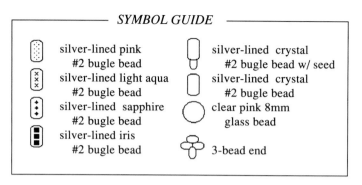

silver-lined pink
#2 bugle bead

silver-lined light aqua
#2 bugle bead

silver-lined sapphire
#2 bugle bead

silver-lined iris
#2 bugle bead

silver-lined crystal
#2 bugle bead w/ seed

silver-lined crystal
#2 bugle bead

clear pink 8mm
glass bead

3-bead end

BARGELLO PIN PATTERN

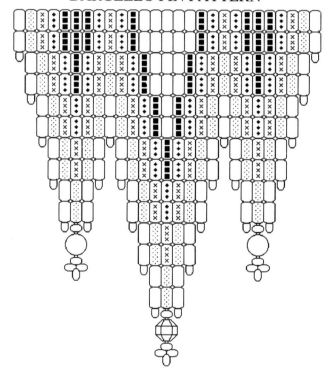

BAR GUIDE

clear pink 8mm
glass bead

frosted amethyst 10mm
donut-shaped rondelle

silver-lined crystal 10/0

AB finished transparent
sappire 6/0

silver-lined crystal
#2 bugle bead

NOEL & CHRISTMAS TREE PINS

NOEL PIN

Materials

11/0 seed beads:
  80 silver-lined amber
  99 opaque lustered red
  176 transparent dark green
  172 opaque lustered white

2" x 4" fabric piece for backing
2" x 4" lightweight cardboard piece
1½" pinback

Directions

1. Weave design piece according to Noel Pin pattern.

2. Make edging around foundation; see pattern.

3. Attach backing fabric and lightweight cardboard to foundation.

4. Sew pinback.

NOEL PIN PATTERN

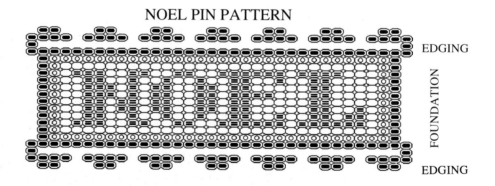

EDGING

FOUNDATION

EDGING

SYMBOL GUIDE

◉ opaque lustered red 11/0
◉ transparent dark green 11/0
○ opaque lustered white 11/0
◎ silver-lined amber 11/0

CHRISTMAS TREE PIN

Materials

11/0 seed beads:
- 237 opaque lustered red
- 133 transparent dark green
- 142 silver-lined amber
- 203 opaque lustered white

2" x 4" fabric piece for backing
2" x 4" lightweight cardboard piece
1½" pinback

Directions

1. Weave design piece according to Christmas Tree Pin pattern.

2. Make edging around foundation; see pattern.

3. Attach backing fabric and lightweight cardboard to foundation.

4. Sew pinback.

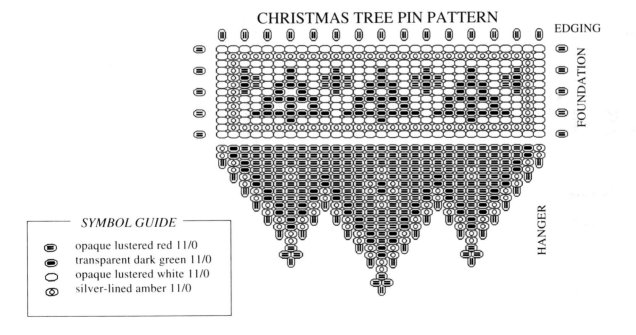

CHRISTMAS TREE PIN PATTERN

EDGING

FOUNDATION

HANGER

SYMBOL GUIDE

- opaque lustered red 11/0
- transparent dark green 11/0
- opaque lustered white 11/0
- silver-lined amber 11/0

 COPPER BARRETTE

COPPER BARRETTE

Materials

11/0 seed beads:
   156 Ceylon pale lavender
   72 metallic light green
   18 transparent rainbow dark green
   24 metallic pink
   15 transparent rainbow light sapphire
   222 metallic copper

1" x 4" lightweight cardboard piece
1" x 4" fabric piece for backing
3" barrette blank

Directions

1. Weave foundation design according to Copper Barrette pattern.

2. Make picots at top and bottom edge; see pattern.

3. Apply backing fabric and lightweight cardboard.

4. Sew barrette blank.

COPPER BARRETTE PATTERN

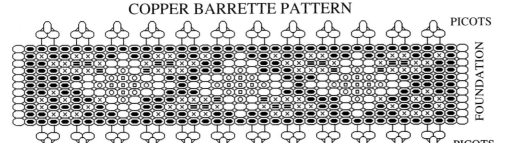

PICOTS

FOUNDATION

PICOTS

SYMBOL GUIDE

- ◉ metallic copper 11/0
- ◯ Ceylon pale lavender 11/0
- ⊗ metallic light green 11/0
- ▤ transparent rainbow dark green 11/0
- ◎ metallic pink 11/0
- ▣ transparent rainbow light sapphire 11/0

MILITARY BAR

MILITARY BAR

Materials

11/0 seed beads:
- 362 Ceylon pale lavender
- 74 color-lined transparent iris
- 54 Ceylon aqua
- 132 antique metallic dark green
- 41 antique metallic brown
- 36 metallic dark champagne
- 362 metallic light champagne

1" x 3" fabric piece for backing
1" x 3" lightweight cardboard piece
1½" pinback

Directions

1. Weave entire piece according to Military Bar pattern.

2. Apply backing fabric and lightweight cardboard to foundation.

3. Sew pinback.

SYMBOL GUIDE

- ◉ antique metallic dark green 11/0
- ◐ antique metallic brown 11/0
- ⊜ metallic dark champagne 11/0
- ⬓ color-lined transparent iris 11/0
- ◎ Ceylon aqua 11/0
- ⊗ metallic light champagne 11/0
- ○ Ceylon pale lavender 11/0

MILITARY BAR PATTERN

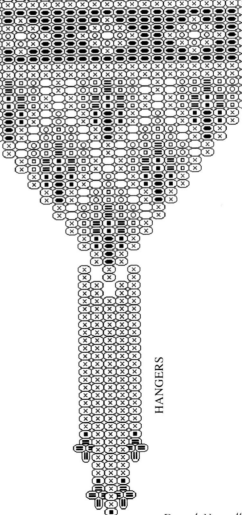

FOUNDATION

HANGERS

Chapter Two

BEAD CARD STITCHING GENERAL INSTRUCTIONS

Bead Card

Bead card stitching is a beadwork technique in which beads are sewn directly to the surface of a bead card. Bead cards can be any form of lightweight cardboard such as heavyweight construction paper or a manila folder, depending on the stiffness you desire.

Patterns

All bead card stitching patterns need to be transferred to the surface of a bead card. You will need the following tools: tracing paper, carbon paper and a writing utensil with a sharp point.

Lay the tracing paper over the pattern and trace all information. Lay carbon paper, carbon-side down, on the surface of the bead card. Lay traced pattern on carbon paper. Re-trace all pattern information to bead card.

Needles

Traditional beading needles are not well suited for bead card stitching. A #9 embroidery needle is ideal when working with seed beads size 11 or larger. For some finely drilled stones and pearls, a #10 quilting needle is recommended.

Removing Unwanted Beads

If you wish to remove beads from a section that is nearly complete, break them off with a medium-size, all-purpose plier.

Thread Types

Ordinary mercerized cotton sewing thread is recommended for most bead card stitching. Choose a neutral color that is similar in theme to your bead design. It is nearly impossible to stitch without a little thread showing between the beads, so try to minimize the distraction by using compatible thread.

Light nylon may be used, but it has greater bulk than ordinary sewing thread and should be restricted to uses where strength is a consideration. If you are using a lot of valuable stones or your beaded piece is supporting any weight, nylon may be a necessary choice.

Fine silk or cotton embroidery floss are good choices for use in bead card stitching. Separate the plies of cotton 6-ply embroidery floss and use only one ply at a time.

Metallic threads are not recommended because the surface fiber tends to fray and ravel. When pulling metallic thread through a tight-fitting bead, fibers will bunch up around the bead opening.

Thread Hints

Soaping or waxing the thread keeps it from tangling. Run the thread across the surface of the soap or wax, then pull the thread between your fingertips to remove any excess.

About Beads

Although most beads are machine manufactured, it is essentially a hand-making process. There is a tremendous amount of variation from one bead to the next in each of the standard bead sizes. These odd-shaped beads can be beneficial and charming when used in some designs. However, to avoid frustration, when the hole in a bead is so tight it does not slip easily over the needle, discard the bead.

About Mosaic Beading

Mosaic beading is a variation of bead card stitching where each bead is carefully placed in a certain position to achieve a realistic or pictorial effect. Each bead or row of beads is specifically marked with a symbol. The proper color of bead is placed directly over its symbol on the card. The beads may be sewn on in long strings that are then couched down to anchor them to the card, or they may be individually sewn in place. It is a good idea to sew on strings or lines of beads where indicated for two reasons. First, it is a great deal faster than applying each individual bead, and second, it causes less wear and tear on the card because there are fewer holes. Of course, each bead will vary a bit in terms of size, so you may not be able to exactly match the placement shown on the card. If you can, try selecting the bead to match the space. If you notice that there are many odd-shaped or flat or narrow or wide beads, set them aside for possible use when filling in odd-shaped spaces. Your own best judgment will be your best guide when deciding where to place odd-shaped beads.

Be careful when trimming the excess card from mosaic designs because you may accidentally cut a long string of beads at the edge.

Certain symbols are used to show bead placement; see Diagram A.

- ▬▫✕⭕▬ indicates a string or line of beads
- ▫ ✕ ⭕ indicates an individual bead and direction
- (✕) ▬(✕)▬ indicates that a space or line shoud be filled with the color in parentheses

Other symbols such as those for pearls or chips will be given in the Symbol Guide for each design.

DIAGRAM A

Couching

Couching is a sewing technique used to anchor objects to any surface. With thread, bring needle up at 1, down at 2. Repeat to attach entire length as desired; see Diagram B.

DIAGRAM B

Slipstitch

Slipstitch is an almost invisible stitch used to join edges. Using a single strand of thread knotted at one end, insert needle at 1 and bring out at 2, picking up a few threads. Slide needle under the folded edge of the fabric ¼", bringing it out at 3 on edge; see Diagram C.

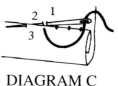

DIAGRAM C

Fusing

To fuse backing fabric to beaded projects, you will need a thick white towel, stitched bead card, fusible webbing with paper removed, fabric, a sheet of clean, white paper and an iron.

Layer and center the components; see Diagram D. Press the iron down flat for five seconds. Shift the iron and press for two seconds more to eliminate any steam holes. Allow the piece to cool completely. With nail scissors, trim excess card and fabric. Run a thin line of diluted white glue around entire outside edge to secure.

IRON

CLEAN, WHITE PAPER

FABRIC RIGHT-SIDE UP

FUSIBLE WEBBING WITH PAPER REMOVED

BEAD CARD FACE DOWN

WHITE TOWEL

DIAGRAM D

Sewing Seed Beads

For small areas and tight curves, it is best to sew on each bead individually. Poke a hole in the card with the needle in the desired location, and bring the thread from back to front. Slip the bead over the needle, and let it slide all the way down the thread until it rests on the card in the desired place. Bring the needle back through the card right in the same hole or very close by so the bead is secured to the card; see Diagram E.

SAME HOLE

TWO HOLES

DIAGRAM E

For gentle curves and outlines, seed beads may be sewn on two at a time; see Diagram F. Poke a hole through the card about two bead lengths forward on the stitching line (hole A). Bring the needle up from back to front. Slip two beads on the needle, letting them slide all the way down the thread until they are on their round sides on the stitching line. Bring the needle down through the card from front to back (hole B) so the two beads are secured. Poke another hole in the stitching line about two bead lengths forward (hole C). Bring the needle up from back to front and slip on two more beads. Slide them to the card, and bring the needle from front to back in the first hole made (hole A). Repeat these steps for the length of the line.

DIAGRAM F

Backtracking

After completing a line of seed beads, fortify the line with backtracking. Bring the needle up just past the last bead in the line, and run the thread back through all the beads in the line. Just after the last bead, bring the needle to the back of the card and secure the thread. This is especially important for outlines around the outside edge of a design. If the beads being backtracked have very fine holes, it may be necessary to use a #10 needle. It will help to run through only three beads at a time, particularly if the line is curved. Keep running through until all the beads in one line are joined together by a single thread; see Diagram G. Tighten it until the line is smooth and neat (but not so tight that there is puckering).

BACKTRACKING THREAD

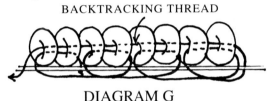

DIAGRAM G

For filling large areas, you may sew several beads at one time, provided they are anchored with small stitches along the length of the line (similar to the needlecraft technique known as couching). Bring the needle up at your chosen starting place and slip on several beads, laying them against the card to see if they fill the desired space comfortably; see Diagram H. Small gaps in the beads will not be noticeable, but large gaps and puckering will not be attractive in the finished work. Try to space the beads so they touch each other gently, but are not crowded. Cramming six beads into a five-bead length will be far more noticeable than the tiny gaps that naturally occur between the rounded edges of beads sewn close to each other.

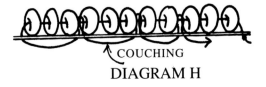

COUCHING

DIAGRAM H

Note: The techniques just described are used when sewing seed beads in sizes 8/0 through 16/0. Larger seed beads, especially E-beads (size 6/0) and pony beads (sizes 5/0 and 4/0), are sewn on individually because of their weight and larger size. Outlines of E-beads and pony beads should be backtracked with thread of a closely coordinated color because the thread can show in the relatively larger gap between beads.

Sewing Bugle Beads

Bugle beads are almost always sewn on individually. Place the unsewn bugle bead on the card in approximately the desired placement and poke a hole at one end. Bring the needle from back to front in this hole, then slip on the bugle bead, allowing it to rest against the card. Bring the needle to the back of the card at the other end of the bead and pull until the bead rests firmly against the card; see Diagram I.

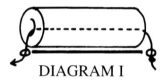

DIAGRAM I

A long line of bugle beads placed end-to-end may be sewn on at one time, provided you anchor the line to the card in several places; see Diagram J. You may want to backtrack the line to firm it up and stabilize it. Since some bugle beads have extremely fine holes, you will probably need to use a #10 quilting needle to backtrack bugle beads. You may have to run though each bead individually when backtracking.

DIAGRAM J

Large bugle beads (#5 and longer) may be sewn on individually as just described. One concern in sewing on any bugle bead, but especially larger ones, is the possibility that the cut end of the glass tube will cut or fray your thread. This is one reason why the thread is never tightened to the point of puckering. When bugle beads are sewn in a fan-shaped area, there will be small gaps between them in some places; see Diagram K. Ignore these spaces, as they will not be particularly noticeable in your finished piece. If they are truly bothersome to you, lightly paint on a thin wash of pale gray watercolor using a small brush. This will soften the appearance of the card between the beads.

SMALL GAPS

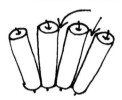

DIAGRAM K

Sewing Crystals

Crystals are sewn on so one of the cut facets lies flat against the card. Place the unsewn crystal on the card in its desired position, and poke a hole at one end. Bring the needle up from back to front through this hole, and slip the crystal on, allowing it to rest against the card in its final position. Bring the needle from front to back at the other end of the crystal; see Diagram L.

DIAGRAM L

Very small crystals (4mm or 5mm) can essentially be treated much as seed beads are treated. They can be sewn on in lines and backtracked or sewn on individually, depending on the final position. Larger crystals (6mm to 12mm) require some additional treatment such as a cross-stitch. Stitch up from lower left, then slip on crystal and bring needle down through card at upper right. Secure crystal by returning thread through crystal, lower right to upper left; see Diagram M.

TOP VIEW

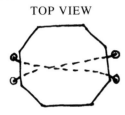

DIAGRAM M

Since there will be some thread visible at each end of the crystal, you may choose to slip on one or two small seed beads prior to slipping on the crystal. Then use one or two small seed beads at the other end of the thread as well; see Diagram N.

DIAGRAM N

Sewing Freshwater Pearls

Pearls have extremely fine holes, and you will have to use a #10 quilting needle. Check each pearl to see that it will slip over the needle before marking the card for it. Position it unsewn on the card as desired, and poke a hole at one end. Bring the needle up from back to front, then slip the pearl on, allowing it to rest on the card; see Diagram O. Note that most freshwater pearls have one side that is slightly flattened. This side should be touching the card and the attractive, rounded surface should face up. It is nearly impossible to backtrack all freshwater pearls.

If they are used in a continuous line, sew them on carefully to insure an attractive appearance.

DIAGRAM O

Sewing Semi-Precious Chips

Most semi-precious chips are drilled though the short side. Position the chip as desired unsewn on the card. Push the needle thought its hole, poking a hole in the card below. Bring the needle from back to front in this hole and slip the chip over the needle until the chip rests flat against the card. Slide one small seed bead over the needle, then insert the needle back through the chip hole. Pull it tight until the small seed bead acts as an anchor on the top surface of the chip; see Diagram P.

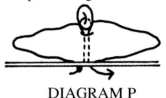

DIAGRAM P

Sewing Odd-Shaped Beads

In general, the shape of the bead determines which method of sewing will be best. If a bead is donut-shaped, it will probably be best sewn using the technique used for semi-precious chips. Long narrow beads may be treated in a similar manner to bugle beads. Faceted or large round beads can be sewn on much like faceted crystals. Below are examples of how to deal with odd beads; see Diagram Q.

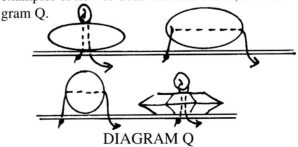

DIAGRAM Q

FREDDY the FISH

FREDDY the FISH

Materials

6mm cupped sequins:
  18 purple
  Nine magenta
  Eight rose
One freshwater pearl
One genuine amazonite chip
#2 silver-lined bugle beads:
  15 light aqua
  56 sapphire
  42 pink

11/0 seed beads:
  258 opaque lustered pale green
  18 color-lined hot pink
  221 metallic gold
3" x 3" gold leather piece
3" x 3" fabric piece for backing
3" x 6" fusible webbing piece
1½" pinback

Directions

1. Transfer Body and Fin patterns on page 78 to bead card.

2. Cut fins from leather and fusible webbing.

3. Position and fuse leather fin pieces on bead card front.

4. Sew lines of metallic gold 11/0 seed beads. Backtrack all lines.

5. Sew lines of all hot pink and pale green 11/0 seed beads.

6. Sew bugle beads. Note that some bugle beads are sewn directly over leather fins. Refer to pattern for placement because you will not see pattern lines through leather.

7. Sew freshwater pearl.

8. Sew amazonite chip on central leather shape.

9. To create scale effect, overlap and sew rose, magenta and purple sequins. Trim sequins to fit odd spaces in pattern, being careful not to cut holes. Anchor all sequins with metallic gold 11/0 seed beads.

10. Fill spaces with opaque lustered pale green 11/0 seed beads.

11. Fuse backing fabric to stitched bead card.

12. With nail scissors, trim excess card/fabric from edges carefully. If needed, slightly trim edges of leather pieces to make smooth edges.

13. Sew pinback.

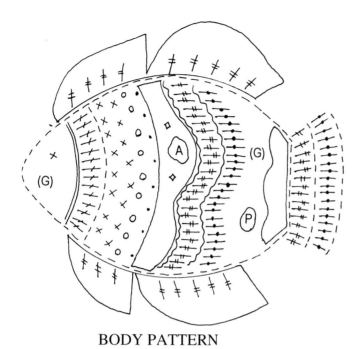

BODY PATTERN

The designer has granted permission to photocopy patterns found in this book.

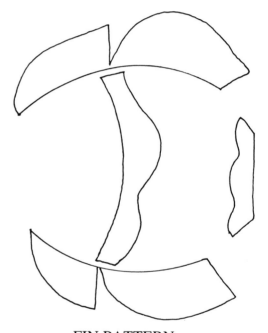

FIN PATTERN

SYMBOL GUIDE

‡	silver-lined sapphire #2 bugle bead
⊬	silver-lined light aqua #2 bugle bead
|	silver-lined pink #2 bugle bead
•	rose 6mm cupped sequin
○	magenta 6mm cupped sequin
×	purple 6mm cupped sequin
Ⓟ	freshwater pearl
Ⓐ	genuine amazonite chip
□	single color-lined hot pink 11/0
／	line of color-lined hot pink 11/0
(G)	fill with opaque lustered pale green 11/0
– – –	line of metallic gold 11/0

JUNE

sun	mon	tues	wed	thurs	fri	sat
					1	2	3
4	5	6	7	8	9	10
11	12	13	14	15	16	17

PURPLE FLORAL BELT

PURPLE FLORAL BELT

Materials

11/0 seed beads:
  728 opaque lustered cream
  498 Ceylon pink
  352 Ceylon orchid
  155 color-lined purple
  66 deep blue purple
  21 transparent dark blue

½ yard of lightweight fabric (silk, rayon, taffeta) for belt
2" length of 1" Velcro
5" x 5" bead card
5" x 5" fabric piece for backing
5" x 5" fusible webbing piece
5" x 5" heavyweight cardboard piece

Directions

1. Transfer Floral pattern on page 81 to bead card.

2. Sew lines of opaque lustered cream seed beads. Backtrack all lines.

3. Sew lines of additional colors, starting with lightest and working toward darkest.

4. Fill center space with amethyst chips, anchoring with deep blue-purple seed beads.

5. Fuse backing fabric to stitched bead card.

6. With nail scissors, trim excess card/fabric from edges carefully; set aside.

7. Cut heavyweight cardboard to size of trimmed design piece.

8. Cut 6" circle from belt fabric. Center heavyweight cardboard piece on wrong side of belt fabric. Wrap and glue edges around cardboard piece, pulling snugly and notching as needed so fabric lies flat.

9. With wrong sides facing, center and stitch beaded design piece to covered heavyweight cardboard piece; set aside.

10. Trim elastic to fit loosely around waist. From belt fabric, cut two 5" x length of trimmed elastic. For a tighter gather on belt, three strips may be used.

11. Sew lengths together at short ends, forming one long strip. Fold strip in half lengthwise with right sides facing and long raw edges aligned. Stitch long raw edges together with ½" seam allowance forming a tube; see Diagram A. Turn.

12. Feed elastic through tube, gathering fabric to accommodate the entire piece of elastic; see Diagram B. Pin or stitch ends so elastic does not slip back into tube. Fold raw fabric ends under; see Diagram C. Slipstitch ends.

13. Center and sew beaded design piece to one end of belt. Sew Velcro piece on belt back behind beaded design piece. Sew corresponding Velcro piece on belt front at opposite end.

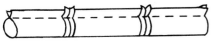

DIAGRAM A

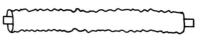

DIAGRAM B

DIAGRAM C

─────────── *SYMBOL GUIDE* ───────────

— opaque lustered cream 11/0

—•— alternate opaque lustered cream and Ceylon pink 11/0

—○— Ceylon pink 11/0

—⊩— alternate Ceylon pink and orchid 11/0

—✕— Ceylon orchid 11/0

—⊟— alternate orchid and color-lined purple 11/0

—●— color-lined purple 11/0

—▲— alternate color-lined purple and deep blue purple 11/0

—⊞— deep blue purple 11/0

—⊪— alternate deep blue purple and transparent dark blue 11/0

—◗— transparent dark blue 11/0

A fill with genuine amethyst chips anchored with deep blue purple 11/0

FLORAL PATTERN

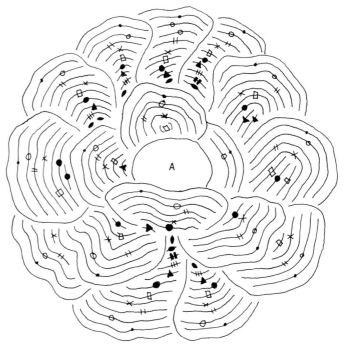

MANDELLA PIN

MANDELLA PIN

Materials

10/0 opaque seed beads:
  336 pink
  96 light amethyst
  72 medium blue
  48 aqua
  40 lime
52 silver-lined amber 11/0 seed beads
24 silver-lined amber 12/0 two-cut
  beads

24 silver-lined amber #3 bugle beads
Eight opaque coral 6mm rondelles
One opaque aqua 10mm rondelle
Eight lustered dark purple 6/0 seed beads
Eight freshwater pearls
3" x 3" bead card
3" x 3" fabric piece for backing
3" x 3" fusible webbing piece
1½" pinback

Directions

1. Transfer Mandella Pin pattern to bead card.

2. Sew all rondelles, anchoring with silver-lined amber 11/0 seed beads.

3. Sew circular line of silver-lined amber 11/0 seed beads. Sew bugle beads and freshwater pearls.

4. Sew lustered dark purple 6/0 seed beads, anchoring with silver-lined amber 11/0 seed beads.

5. Fill the area surrounding each freshwater pearl out to bugle beads with opaque pink 10/0 seed beads.

6. Sew individual 12/0 silver-lined two-cut beads. Sew lines of opaque pink 10/0 seed beads. Backtrack lines.

7. Sew lines of light amethyst, medium blue, aqua and lime opaque 10/0 seed beads.

8. Fuse backing fabric to stitched bead card.

9. With nail scissors, trim excess card/fabric from edges carefully.

10. Sew pinback.

MANDELLA PIN PATTERN

SYMBOL GUIDE

```
······  lines of silver-lined amber 11/0
  I     individual silver-lined amber
          12/0 two-cut beads
- - -   lines of lime 10/0
_____  lines of pink 10/0
∿∿∿     lines of light amethyst 10/0
⌒⌒      lines of medium blue 10/0
_____  lines of aqua 10/0
(•)     opaque aqua 10mm rondelle
(○)     opaque coral 6mm rondelle
(⊙)     lustered dark purple 6/0
(P)     freshwater pearls
↓       silver-lined #3 bugle beads
```

DOGWOOD MOSAIC PIN

DOGWOOD MOSAIC PIN

Materials

11/0 seed beads:

    42 opaque dark green

    50 opaque dark rust

    54 iris purple

    62 opaque lustered red

    311 opaque rose

    219 opaque pale olive

    89 opaque lustered cream

17 metallic gold 6/0 seed beads

3" x 4" bead card

3" x 4" fabric for backing

3" x 4" fusible webbing piece

1½" pinback

Directions

1. Transfer Dogwood Mosaic Pin pattern to bead card.

2. Sew metallic gold 6/0 seed beads, anchoring with opaque pale olive 11/0 seed beads.

3. Sew remaining lines of beads, anchoring with couching.

4. Fill with individual beads according to pattern.

5. Fuse backing fabric to stitched bead card.

6. With nail scissors, trim excess card/fabric from edges carefully.

7. Sew pinback.

SYMBOL GUIDE

‖‖	opaque dark green 11/0	✕	opaque lustered red 11/0
●	opaque dark rust 11/0	O	opaque rose 11/0
▉	iris purple 11/0	•	opaque pale olive 11/0
◯	metallic gold 6/0	ǀ	opaque lustered cream 11/0

**DOGWOOD MOSAIC PIN
PATTERN**

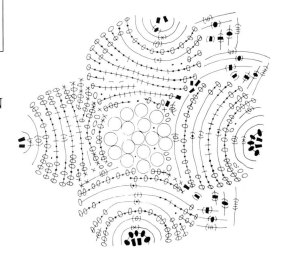

For your convenience, an enlarged version of this pattern is found on page 137.

 MOSAIC SEA SHELL

MOSAIC SEA SHELL

Materials

11/0 seed beads:
    104 transparent iris dark amber
    406 color-lined tan
    592 opaque lustered cream
    30 iris purple
Seven freshwater pearls

14 opaque lustered cream 6/0 seed beads
3" x 4" bead card
3" x 4" fabric piece for backing
3" x 4" fusible webbing piece
1½" pinback

Directions

1. Transfer Mosaic Sea Shell pattern to bead card.

2. Sew freshwater pearls.

3. Sew opaque lustered cream 6/0 seed beads, anchoring with opaque lustered cream 11/0 seed beads.

4. Sew lines of beads according to pattern, couching lines to keep them in position.

5. Fill remaining spaces with individual beads according to pattern.

6. Fuse backing fabric to stitched bead card.

7. With nail scissors, trim excess card/fabric from edges carefully.

8. Sew pinback.

MOSAIC SEA SHELL PATTERN

SYMBOL GUIDE

●	iris purple 11/0
▯	transparent iris dark amber 11/0
0	color-lined tan 11/0
•	opaque lustered cream 11/0
Ⓟ	freshwater pearl
◯	opaque lustered cream 6/0

For your convenience, an enlarged version of this pattern is found on page 138.

CRYSTAL CROSS PIN

CRYSTAL CROSS PIN

Materials

Four 6mm crystals
One 14mm crystal
Four freshwater pearls
55 transparent amethyst 8/0 seed beads
107 silver-lined crystal 11/0 seed beads
101 silver-lined crystal #2 bugle beads
11/0 two-cut beads:
   83 opaque light blue
   85 transparent medium blue
   37 silver-lined medium green

3" x 4" bead card
3" x 4" fabric piece for backing
3" x 4" fusible webbing piece
1½" pinback

Directions

1. Transfer Crystal Cross Pin pattern to bead card.

2. Sew all crystals.

3. Sew freshwater pearls, amethyst 8/0 seed beads and bugle beads.

4. Sew silver-lined crystal 11/0 seed beads around outside edge. Backtrack entire edge.

5. Fill center area with 11/0 two-cut beads.

6. Fuse backing fabric stitched bead card.

7. With nail scissors, trim excess card/fabric from edges carefully.

8. Sew pinback.

CRYSTAL CROSS PIN PATTERN

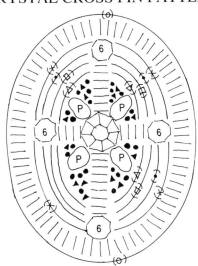

SYMBOL GUIDE

-⊙- silver-lined crystal 11/0
✕ transparent amethyst 8/0
• line of opaque light blue 11/0 two-cut beads
□ line of transparent medium blue 11/0 two-cut beads
△ line of silver-lined medium green 11/0 two-cut beads
● single silver-lined medium green 11/0 two-cut bead
▲ single transparent medium blue 11/0 two-cut bead
Ⓟ freshwater pearl
⑥ 6mm crystal
⊛ 14mm crystal
| silver-lined crystal #2 bugle bead

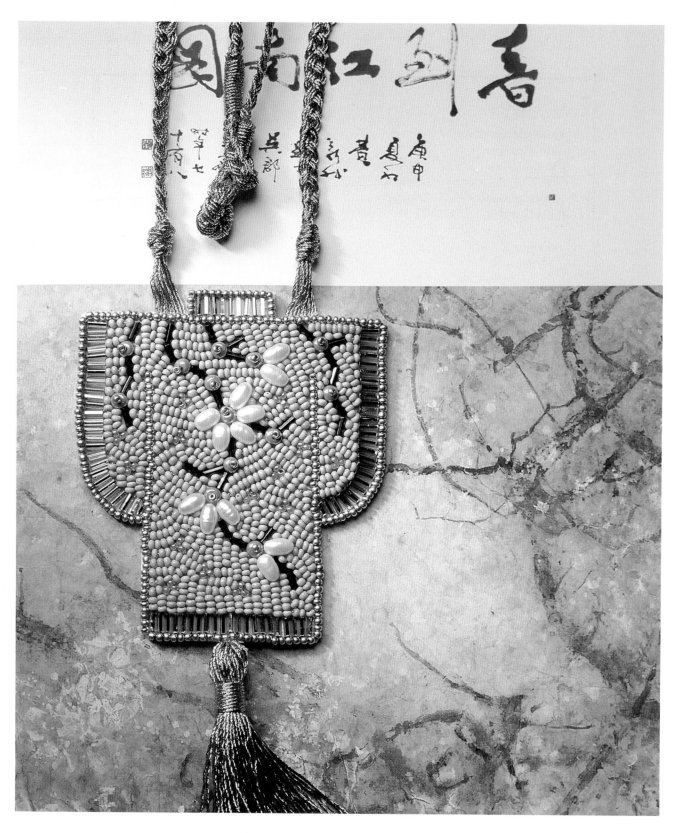

KIMONO NECKLACE

KIMONO NECKLACE

Materials

11/0 seed beads:
   254 metallic gold
   42 Ceylon amethyst
   798 opaque pink
13 lustered aqua 6/0 seed beads
30 iris blue #2 bugle beads

83 silver-lined aqua #2 bugle beads
12 freshwater pearls
16 yards of metallic gold fiber
4" x 5" bead card
4" x 5" fabric piece for backing
4" x 5" fusible webbing piece

Directions

1. Transfer Kimono pattern on page 92 to bead card.

2. Sew lines of metallic gold 11/0 seed beads.

3. Sew silver-lined aqua bugle beads.

4. Sew lustered aqua 6/0 seed beads, anchoring with metallic gold 11/0 seed beads.

5. Sew freshwater pearls, iris blue bugle beads and Ceylon amethyst 11/0 seed beads.

6. Fill background with opaque pink 11/0 seed beads.

7. Trim top edge and neck of design carefully; leave sides and bottom intact.

8. Make two necklace braids from ten 15" lengths each of metallic gold fiber; see Diagram A.

KNOT ONE END   LOOP ONE END

DIAGRAM A

9. Attach loose ends of necklace braids to top edge of kimono sleeves with small invisible stitches.

10. Fuse backing fabric to stitched bead card.

11. With nail scissors, trim excess bead card/fabric from remaining edges carefully.

12. Make bottom tassel using 35 6" pieces of metallic gold fiber; see Diagram B. Sew tassel to bottom center edge.

DIAGRAM B

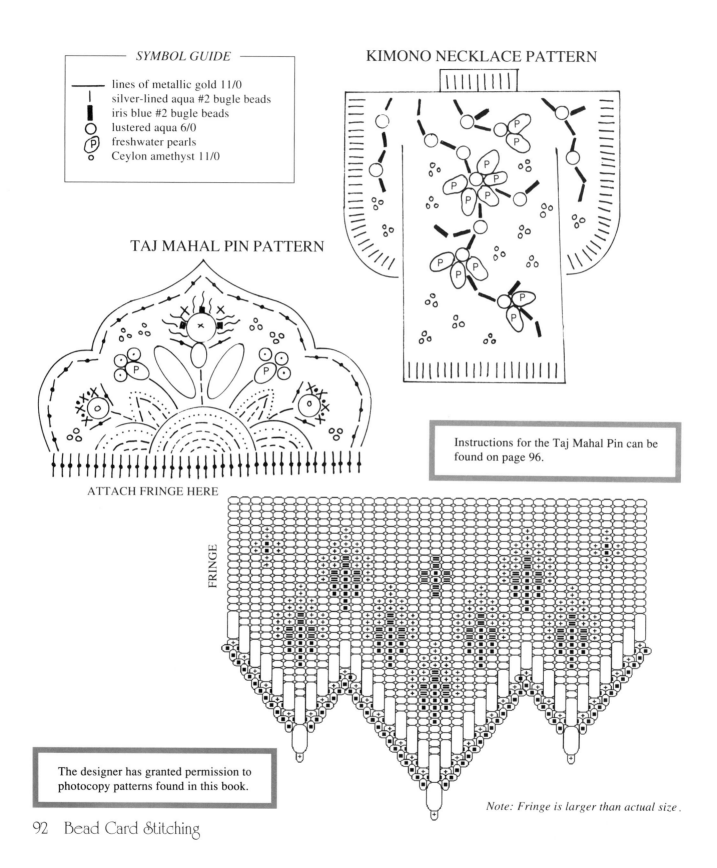

The designer has granted permission to photocopy patterns found in this book.

MOSAIC MONARCH NECKLACE OR PIN

MOSAIC MONARCH NECKLACE or PIN

Materials

11/0 seed beads:
   406 metallic gold
   163 metallic bronze
   179 metallic copper
   376 transparent rainbow aqua
Four freshwater pearls
19 metallic gold 6/0 seed beads
Two turquoise chips
Two tiger eye chips
25 satin-finished light amber #3
   bugle beads
Five medium amber 4mm x 6mm
   glass tubes
Three amber 6mm x 10mm beads
   (substitute amber-colored glass or
   carnelian beads)
4" x 6" bead card

4" x 6" fabric piece for backing
4" x 6" fusible webbing piece
1½" pinback for pin

Additional materials for necklace:
One large amber (or substitute) bead,
   approximately 10mm x 14mm
11/0 seed beads:
   912 transparent rainbow aqua
   27 metallic copper
   39 metallic bronze
   49 metallic gold
Two metallic gold 6/0 seed beads
Two gold-finished end caps
One gold-finished clasp
#0 nylon thread

Directions

1. Transfer Mosaic Monarch pattern on page 95 to bead card.

2. Sew amber beads (or substitute) to form center body of butterfly.

3. Sew lines of metallic gold 11/0 seed beads. Backtrack all lines.

4. Sew metallic gold 6/0 seed beads, anchoring with metallic copper 11/0 seed beads.

5. Sew turquoise and tiger eye chips, freshwater pearls, amber glass tubes and bugle beads.

6. Fill background areas according to pattern.

7. Sew lines of metallic gold, metallic bronze and metallic copper 11/0 seed beads; see pattern.

8. Fuse backing fabric to stitched bead card.

9. With nail scissors, trim excess card/fabric from edges carefully.

10. For necklace, use #0 nylon thread to string beads. String a total of 8" of transparent rainbow

aqua 11/0 between the amber bead and the end cap on all three strands before running it through the end cap and clasp; see diagram. Make sure all three strands are of equal length. Attach bottom drop according to pattern, making sure it can swing freely.

For pin: *Sew pinback to stitched bead card.*

DIAGRAM

BOTTOM DROP

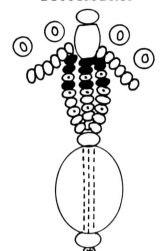

SYMBOL GUIDE

⊙	metallic gold 6/0 anchored with metallic copper 11/0
=	satin-finished light amber #3 bugle bead
o	metallic gold 6/0 sewn with side down
⬭	freshwater pearl
⬮	4mm x 6mm glass tube
⬚	tiger eye chip anchored with metallic copper 11/0
✶	turquoise chip anchored with metallic bronze 11/0
✳	large amber bead or substitute
——	outline of metallic gold 11/0
- - - -	line of alternating metallic gold and bronze 11/0
— —	line of metallic bronze 11/0
......	line of alternating metallic bronze and coppper 11/0
(x)	fill with lines of metallic copper 11/0
(A)	fill with transparent rainbow aqua 11/0

DROP SYMBOLS

○	metallic gold 11/0
⊙	metallic bronze 11/0
●	metallic copper 11/0

Instructions for the Paisley Pin can be found on page 99.

SYMBOL GUIDE

⌒	lines of metallic gold 11/0
⌒ (dashed)	lines of transparent rainbow dark amber 11/0
⌒ (dotted)	lines of transparent rainbow light amber 11/0
⊙	metallic gold 6/0 anchored with metallic gold 11/0
C	carnelian chip
(▲)	fill with metallic dark copper 11/0
(x)	fill with transparent rainbow light amber 11/0
(O)	fill with opaque lustered cream 11/0
(=)	fill with iris purple 11/0

MOSAIC MONARCH PATTERN

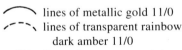

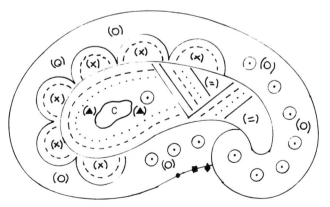

PAISLEY PIN PATTERN

TAJ MAHAL PIN

Materials

11/0 seed beads:
- 607 silver-lined amber
- 187 silver-lined dark amethyst
- 122 silver-lined dark green
- 262 silver-lined aqua
- 100 silver-lined amber #3 bugle beads
- Nine silver-lined aqua #2 bugle beads
- Eight clear amethyst 8/0 seed beads
- Six freshwater pearls

- Six lustered pink 6/0 seed beads
- One amethyst 10mm rondelle
- Two amethyst 6mm rondelles
- Two dark green acrylic navette beads
- 4" x 6" cream satin piece
- 4" x 6" bead card
- 4" x 6" fabric piece for backing
- Two 4" x 6" fusible webbing pieces
- 1½" pinback

Directions

1. Transfer Taj Mahal Pin pattern on page 92 to bead card. Retrace lines with dark ink pen; let dry.

2. Fuse satin directly on pattern; lines will show through satin well enough to bead over them.

3. Sew lines of silver-lined amber 11/0 seed beads. Backtrack lines.

4. Sew lines of remaining 11/0 beads. Sew navettes, anchoring with silver-lined aqua 11/0 seed beads. Sew freshwater pearls and rondelles.

6. Sew lustered pink 6/0 seed beads, anchoring with silver-lined dark amethyst 11/0 seed beads.

7. Sew clear amethyst 8/0 seed beads. Sew individual silver-lined amber and aqua 11/0 seed beads.

8. Sew all bugle beads.

9. Fuse backing fabric to stitched bead card.

10. Make fringe, attaching to all bugle beads at lower edge of stitched bead card; see pattern.

11. With nail scissors, trim excess card/fabric from edges, being careful not to cut fringe.

12. Sew pinback.

SYMBOL GUIDE

amethyst 10mm rondelle	silver-lined amber 11/0
amethyst 6mm rondelle	lines of silver-lined amber 11/0
dark green navette	lines of silver-lined aqua 11/0
freshwater pearl	lines of silver-lined dark green 11/0
lustered pink 6/0	lines of silver-lined dark amethyst 11/0
silver-lined aqua #2 bugle bead	freshwater pearl
silver-lined amber #3 bugle bead	silver-lined dark green 11/0
silver-lined dark amethyst 11/0	silver-lined dark amethyst 11/0
clear amethyst 8/0	silver-lined aqua 11/0
silver-lined aqua 11/0	silver-lined amber 11/0

TAJ MAHAL PIN

PAISLEY PIN

PAISLEY PIN

Materials

11/0 seed beads:
   383 metallic gold
   120 transparent rainbow dark amber
   63 transparent rainbow light amber
   47 metallic dark copper
   27 iris purple
   395 opaque lustered cream
11 metallic gold 6/0 seed beads
Six iris purple 6/0 seed beads
One carnelian chip

One transparent amber 12mm faceted
   crystal
One light amber clear glass 10mm round
   bead
One carnelian 8mm bead
2" x 4" bead card
2" x 4" fabric piece for backing
2" x 4" fusible webbing piece
1½" pinback

Directions

1. Transfer Paisley Pin pattern on page 95 to bead card.

2. Sew lines of metallic gold 11/0 seed beads.

3. Sew metallic gold 6/0 seed beads, anchoring with metallic gold 11/0 seed beads.

4. Sew lines of dark amber 11/0 seed beads and light amber 11/0 seed beads.

5. Sew carnelian chip, anchoring with metallic gold 11/0 seed beads.

6. Fill with iris purple 11/0 seed beads, metallic copper 11/0 seed beads and light amber 11/0 seed beads.

7. Make hangers according to pattern below.

8. Fuse backing fabric to stitched bead card.

9. With nail scissors, trim excess card/fabric from edges carefully, taking care not to cut hangers.

10. Sew pinback.

HANGERS

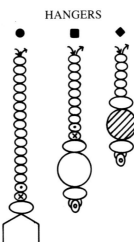

HANGER SYMBOLS

carnelian 8mm bead
light amber clear glass 10mm round bead
transparent amber 12mm faceted crystal
transparent rainbow light amber 11/0
metallic gold 11/0
transparent rainbow dark amber 11/0
iris purple 11/0
iris purple 6/0

SOMEWHERE OVER the RAINBOW

SOMEWHERE OVER the RAINBOW

Materials

11/0 seed beads:
- 138 silver-lined crystal
- 48 opaque lustered pink
- 47 opaque lustered orchid
- 45 opaque lustered lavender
- 41 opaque lustered medium purple
- 39 opaque lustered blue
- 37 opaque lustered aqua
- 32 opaque lustered light green

Five silver 4mm English cut beads
One AB finished 10mm crystal
Two AB finished 6mm crystals
2" x 3" bead card
2" x 3" fabric piece for backing
2" x 3" fusible webbing piece
1½" pinback

Directions

1. Transfer Rainbow pattern to bead card.

2. Sew silver-lined crystal beads all around outside line of card.

3. Fill lines of other color seed beads according pattern.

4. Sew hangers A, B and C according to pattern.

5. Fuse backing fabric to stitched bead card.

6. With nail scissors, trim excess card/fabric from edges carefully.

7. Sew pinback.

HANGER GUIDE

A B C

- ⊕ opaque lustered pink 11/0
- ⊚ opaque lustered orchid 11/0
- ⊟ opaque lustered lavender 11/0
- ⊡ opaque lustered medium purple 11/0
- ⊗ opaque lustered blue 11/0
- ⊚ opaque lustered aqua 11/0
- ⊜ opaque lustered light green 11/0
- ✪ silver 4mm English cut bead
- ✿ AB finished 6mm crystal
- ✸ AB finished 10mm crystal
- ⚘ 3-bead end

SYMBOL GUIDE

- ——— line of silver-lined crystal 11/0
- — — line of opaque lustered pink 11/0
- - - - - line of opaque lustered orchid 11/0
- ∿∿∿ line of opaque lustered lavender 11/0
- —·—·— line of opaque lustered medium purple 11/0
- · · · · · line of opaque lustered blue 11/0
- —··—··— line of opaque lustered aqua 11/0
- ∼∼∼ line of opaque lustered light green 11/0
  silver-lined crystal

RAINBOW PATTERN

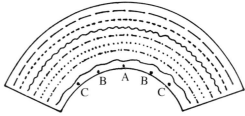

The designer has granted permission to photocopy patterns found in this book.

NEPTUNE BARRETTE

NEPTUNE BARRETTE

Materials

11/0 seed beads:
    325 silver-lined crystal
    362 Ceylon orchid
    206 opaque aqua
    88 opaque medium blue
    52 transparent dark green
    Seven transparent dark blue
One dark green 15mm round acrylic
    faceted stone

One green acrylic 17mm navette-
    shaped faceted sew-on stone
Two freshwater pearls
39 iris #3 bugle beads
4" x 5" bead card
4" x 5" fabric piece for backing
4" x 5" fusible webbing piece
3" barrette blank

Directions

1. Transfer Neptune Barrette pattern to bead card.

2 Sew lines of silver-lined crystal 11/0 seed beads. Backtrack lines.

3. Sew bugle beads.

4. Sew lines of Ceylon orchid 11/0 seed beads.

5. Sew freshwater pearls.

6. Sew navette acrylic stone, anchoring with transparent dark green 11/0 seed beads.

7. Fill lines and individual 11/0 seed beads of all remaining colors.

8. Glue round acrylic faceted stone in place.

9. Fuse backing fabric to stitched bead card.

10. With nail scissors, trim excess card/fabric from edges carefully.

11. Sew barrette blank.

NEPTUNE BARRETTE PATTERN

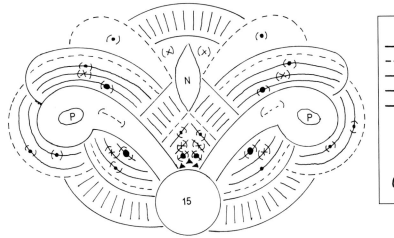

SYMBOL GUIDE

——————— line of silver-lined crystal 11/0
– – – – – line of Ceylon orchid 11/0
—•— line of opaque aqua 11/0
—×— line of opaque medium blue 11/0
—●— line of transparent dark green 11/0
N green acrylic 17mm navette
15 dark green 15mm acrylic facted stone
▲ transparent dark blue 11/0
| iris #3 bugle bead
(P) freshwater pearls

PAINTED LADY COMB

PAINTED LADY COMB

Materials

11/0 seed beads:
  243 Ceylon aqua
  111 color-lined iris
  223 metallic gold
24 metallic gold #2 bugle beads
Five iris #2 bugle beads
Six freshwater pearls

One 14mm–16mm turquoise chip or one
  decorative button for head
3" x 5" bead card
3" x 5" fabric piece for backing
3" x 5" fusible webbing piece
One 2"–2½" hair comb
Double-sided tape

Directions

1. Transfer Painted Lady pattern to bead card.

2. Sew turquoise chip or button, anchoring with metallic gold 11/0 seed bead.

3. Sew lines of gold metallic 11/0 seed beads. Backtrack all lines.

4. Sew metallic gold and iris bugle beads.

5. Sew freshwater pearls.

6. Fill with Ceylon aqua and color-lined iris 11/0 seed beads.

7. Fuse backing fabric to wrong side of stitched bead card.

8. With nail scissors, trim excess card/fabric from edges carefully.

9. Appiy double-sided tape to right side, top edge of comb. Press beaded piece firmly on double-sided tape. Secure with a few small invisible stitches. (Do not depend on tape alone to hold beading to comb.)

PAINTED LADY PATTERN

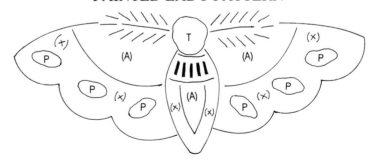

SYMBOL GUIDE

(P) freshwater pearl
— line of metallic gold 11/0
| metallic gold #2 bugle bead
▮ iris #2 bugle bead
(T) turquoise chip
A fill with color-lined iris 11/0
X fill with Ceylon aqua 11/0

The designer has granted permission to photocopy patterns found in this book.

MOSAIC BRIDGE BELT

MOSAIC BRIDGE BELT

Materials

11/0 seed beads:
- 105 metallic gold
- 37 transparent aqua
- 35 Ceylon pale blue
- 45 white-lined
- 44 transparent dark amber
- 117 color-lined tan
- 35 opaque lustered pale green
- 36 transparent rainbow dark green
- 26 transparent rainbow medium green
- 18 opaque bright red (used only to anchor rondelles)

#2 bugle beads:
- 14 silver-lined dark green
- 24 metallic gold
- Nine silver-lined sapphire
- 12 silver-lined aqua
- 14 silver-lined crystal

#1 bugle beads or 11/0 two-cut beads:
- Six silver-lined aqua
- Four silver-lined sapphire

Seven satin-finished dark brown #3 bugle beads

Seven bright yellow 10/0 seed beads

18 bright red 6mm flat rondelles

Six nugget-sized turquoise chips

4" x 4" bead card

4" x 4" fabric piece for backing

4" x 4" fusible webbing piece

4" x 4" heavyweight cardboard piece

⅛ yard of clothesline

½ yard of lightweight fabric (silk, rayon, taffeta) for belt

1 yard of 1½" non-roll elastic

2" length of 1" Velcro

Directions

1. Transfer Mosaic Bridge pattern on page 109 to bead card.

2. Sew circular gold outline just between border and interior design. Backtrack all around design piece.

3. Sew satin-finished dark brown #3 bugle beads on bridge.

4. Sew lines of opaque lustered pale green 11/0 seed beads.

5. Sew transparent rainbow medium and transparent rainbow dark green 11/0 seed beads.

6. Sew silver-lined dark green #2 bugle beads.

7. Sew color-lined tan 11/0 seed beads to fill in bridge.

8. Sew transparent dark amber 11/0 beads to form hill.

9. Sew all sky colors.

10. Sew bugle beads in water area below bridge.

11. Sew on metallic gold #2 bugle beads in border.

12. Sew red 6mm flat rondelles, anchoring with red 11/0 seed beads.

13. Sew turquoise chips, anchoring with transparent medium green 11/0 seed beads.

14. Fuse backing fabric to stitched bead card.

15. With nail scissors, trim excess card/fabric from edges carefully.

16. Cut heavyweight cardboard to size of trimmed design piece.

17. Cut 4" circle from belt fabric. Center heavyweight cardboard piece on wrong side of belt fabric. Wrap and glue edges around cardboard piece, pulling snugly and notching as needed so fabric lies flat.

18. Cut clothesline slightly larger than the circumference of the trimmed design piece.

19. From belt fabric, cut one piece 2" x three times the length of the clothesline.

20. Fold fabric in half lengthwise with wrong sides facing and long raw edges aligned. Stitch long raw edges together with ⅜ " seam allowance; see Diagram A. Do not turn. Feed clothesline through length, gathering fabric until both ends of the clothesline protrude from ends.

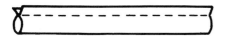

DIAGRAM A

21. Sew clothesline ends together to form a continuous circle; see Diagram B. Fold raw fabric ends

under and slipstitch together; see Diagram C.

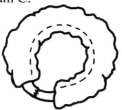

DIAGRAM B

DIAGRAM C

22. Center heavyweight cardboard/fabric circle, right-side down, on gathered circle; see Diagram D. Slipstitch.

DIAGRAM D

23. With wrong sides facing, center and stitch beaded design piece to gathered circle; see Diagram E.

DIAGRAM E

24. Trim elastic to fit loosely around waist. From belt fabric, cut two 5" x length of trimmed

elastic. For a tighter gather on belt, three strips may be used.

25. Sew lengths together at short ends, forming one long strip. Fold strip in half lengthwise with right sides facing and long raw edges aligned. Stitch long raw edges together with ½" seam allowance forming a tube; see Diagram F. Turn.

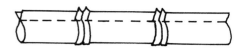

DIAGRAM F

26. Feed elastic through tube, gathering fabric to accommodate the entire piece of elastic; see Diagram G. Pin or stitch ends so elastic does not slip back into tube. Fold raw fabric ends under; see Diagram H. Slipstitch ends.

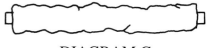

DIAGRAM G

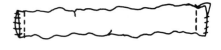

DIAGRAM H

27. Center and sew beaded piece on one end of belt. Sew Velcro piece on belt back behind beaded piece. Sew corresponding Velcro piece on belt front at opposite end.

For your convenience, an enlarged version of this pattern is found on page 139.

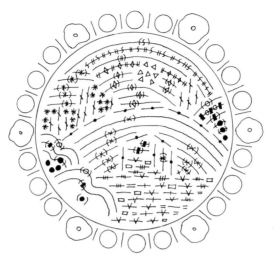

MOSAIC BRIDGE PATTERN

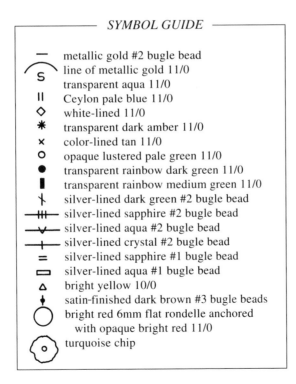

SYMBOL GUIDE

— metallic gold #2 bugle bead
∫S line of metallic gold 11/0
transparent aqua 11/0
‖ Ceylon pale blue 11/0
◇ white-lined 11/0
✳ transparent dark amber 11/0
✕ color-lined tan 11/0
○ opaque lustered pale green 11/0
● transparent rainbow dark green 11/0
▮ transparent rainbow medium green 11/0
⅄ silver-lined dark green #2 bugle bead
‑Ⅲ‑ silver-lined sapphire #2 bugle bead
‑v‑ silver-lined aqua #2 bugle bead
‑+‑ silver-lined crystal #2 bugle bead
= silver-lined sapphire #1 bugle bead
▭ silver-lined aqua #1 bugle bead
△ bright yellow 10/0
♦ satin-finished dark brown #3 bugle beads
◯ bright red 6mm flat rondelle anchored
    with opaque bright red 11/0
⬡ turquoise chip

 MOSAIC TREE SCENE

MOSAIC TREE SCENE

Materials

12/0-13/0 hex beads:
  30 pale blue
  32 medium blue-purple
  53 dark blue-purple
  58 lustered light amethyst
  34 opaque grape (grayish)
  26 opaque dark green
  118 opaque medium green
  120 opaque light green
  11 dark brown
  13 rust
  4 orange
  10 yellow
  43 rose
  45 light gray
  Six white

12/0 three-cut beads:
  403 metallic gold
  120 color-lined dark aqua
  32 iris
  21 satin pale peach
3" x 3" bead card
3" x 3" fabric for backing
3" x 3" fusible webbing piece
1½" pinback

Directions

1. Transfer Mosaic Tree Scene pattern on page 112 to bead card.

2. Sew interior design according to pattern.

3. Sew metallic gold 12/0 three-cut beads.

4. Fill spaces in border with color-lined dark aqua 12/0 three-cut beads.

5. Fuse backing fabric to stitched bead card.

6. With nail scissors, trim excess card/fabric from edges carefully.

7. Sew pinback

For your convenience, an enlarged version
of this pattern is found on page 140.

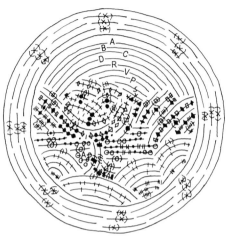

MOSAIC TREE SCENE
PATTERN

SYMBOL GUIDE

I	opaque light green hex bead
◇	opaque medium green hex bead
III	lustered light amethyst hex bead
◆	opaque grape hex bead
■	dark brown hex bead
◻	light gray hex bead
∩	rust hex bead
●	opaque dark green hex bead
A	dark blue-purple hex bead
B	alternate dk blue-purple and medium blue-purple hex beads
C	medium blue-purple hex bead
D	alternate medium blue-purple and rose hex beads
R	rose hex bead
V	alternate rose hex bead and satin pale peach 12/0 three-cut beads
P	satin pale peach 12/0 three-cut bead
S	alternate yellow hex bead and satin pale peach 12/0 three-cut beads
Y	yellow hex bead
▲	orange hex bead
·	pale blue hex bead
O	medium blue-purple hex bead
II	white hex bead
×	color-lined dark aqua 12/0 three-cut bead
——	metallic gold 12/0 three-cut bead

BRIDAL GARTER

BRIDAL GARTER

Materials

136 white opaque lustered 10/0 seed
   beads
Seven AB finished white #3 bugle
   beads
Two 6mm crystals

One 10mm crystal
Ten freshwater pearls
402 color-lined white 11/0 seed beads
16" length of ½" elastic
3" x 32" ivory satin piece

Directions

1. Transfer Bridal Garter pattern on page 115 to bead card.

2. Sew lines of white opaque 10/0 seed beads. Backtrack all lines.

3. Sew bugle beads, crystals and freshwater pearls according to pattern.

4. Fill background with white color-lined 11/0 seed beads.

5. Fuse backing fabric to stitched bead card.

6. With nail scissors, trim excess card/fabric from edges carefully.

7. Make fringes according to pattern. Attach below bugle beads; set aside.

8. Fold ivory satin piece in half lengthwise with right sides facing. Stitch long raw edges together with ½" seam allowance to form tube; see Diagram A. Turn.

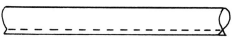

DIAGRAM A

9. Feed elastic through satin tube, gathering satin until ½" protrudes from each end; see Diagram B.

DIAGRAM B

10. Sew ends of elastic together, making sure elastic is not twisted inside the satin tube; see Diagram C.

DIAGRAM C

11. Fold raw ends of satin inside tube and slipstitch together; see Diagram D.

DIAGRAM D

12. Stitch beaded piece firmly to garter over seam.

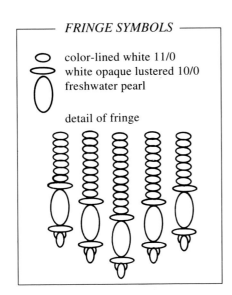

color-lined white 11/0
white opaque lustered 10/0
freshwater pearl

detail of fringe

line of white opaque lustered 10/0
freshwater pearls
10mm crystal
6mm crystal
AB finished white #3 bugle bead

BRIDAL GARTER PATTERN

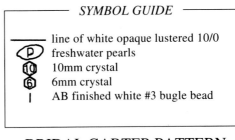

Instructions for the Bridal Tiara can be found on page 117.

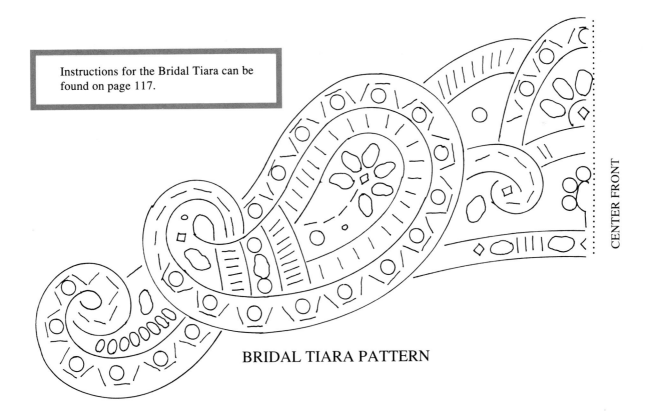

BRIDAL TIARA PATTERN

CENTER FRONT

BRIDAL TIARA

BRIDAL TIARA

Materials

34 freshwater pearls
11 AB finished firepolished 5mm
   crystals
74 AB finished crystal 6/0 seed beads
292 AB finished crystal #2 bugle beads

1322 opaque lustered white 10/0 seed
   beads
5" x 14" bead card
Two 5" x 14" white satin pieces
Two 5" x 14" fusible webbing pieces
Two 2" white hair combs

Directions

1. Transfer Bridal Tiara pattern, on page 115, doubled to bead card. Retrace lines with a dark ink pen; let dry.

2. Fuse one satin piece directly on top of pattern; lines will show through satin well enough to bead over them.

3. Sew lines of opaque lustered white 10/0 seed beads. Backtrack all lines. Sew 5mm crystals, freshwater pearls and bugle beads.

4. Sew AB finished crystal 6/0 seed beads, anchoring with white opaque 10/0 seed beads.

5. Sew AB finished crystal 6/0 seed beads sideways.

6. Fuse remaining satin piece to stitched bead card.

7. With nail scissors, trim excess card/satin from edges carefully.

8. Sew combs to each end of headpiece back.

SYMBOL GUIDE

— line of opaque lustered white 10/0
o single opaque lustered white 10/0
– AB finished crystal #2 bugle bead
⬭ freshwater pearl

◇ AB finished firepolished 5mm crystal
◯ AB finished crystal 6/0 anchored with opaque lustered white 10/0
◍ AB finished crystal 6/0 sewn on side

BRIDAL HAIR COMB

BRIDAL HAIR COMB

Materials

Five freshwater pearls
Ten 6mm crystals
13 AB finished white #3 bugle beads
Eight 4mm x 10mm glass tubes
140 opaque lustered white 10/0 seed
    beads

260 white-lined 11/0 seed beads
3" x 4" bead card
3" x 4" fabric piece for backing
3" x 4" fusible webbing piece
One 2" –2½" white hair comb
Double-sided tape

Directions

1. Transfer Bridal Hair Comb pattern to bead card.

2. Sew lines of white opaque lustered 10/0 seed beads. Backtrack all lines.

3. Sew freshwater pearls, 4mm x 10mm glass tubes, crystals and bugle beads.

4. Sew line of white-lined 11/0 seed beads.

5. Fill side areas with white-lined 11/0 seed beads.

6. Fuse backing fabric to stitched bead card.

7. With nail scissors, trim excess card/fabric from edges carefully.

8. Apply double-sided tape to right side, top edge of comb.

9. Press design piece firmly on double-sided tape. Anchor with a few small invisible stitches. (Do not depend on adhesive alone to hold beading on comb.)

SYMBOL GUIDE

▯	4mm x 10mm glass tube
◯	6mm crystal
Ⓟ	freshwater pearl
⌒	line of opaque lustered white 10/0
∿	line of white-lined 11/0
x	fill with white-lined 11/0
┃	AB finished white #3 bugle bead

BRIDAL HAIR COMB PATTERN

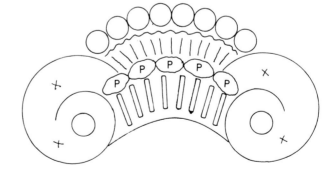

 PEACHY KEEN

PEACHY KEEN

Materials

All beads are 11/0 seed beads.

74 iris green
44 opaque lustered medium green
14 opaque lustered pale green
41 Ceylon pale yellow
149 Ceylon pale gold
204 Ceylon peach
114 color-lined soft red

108 opaque lustered bright orange
16 transparent dark amber
3" x 3" bead card
3" x 3" fabric piece for backing
3" x 3" fusible webbing piece
1½" pinback

Directions

1. Transfer Peach pattern to bead card.

2. Sew all lines of beads and all individual beads according to pattern.

3. Backtrack lines on outside edge of piece.

4. Fuse backing fabric to stitched bead card.

5. With nail scissors, trim excess card/fabric from edges carefully.

6. Sew pinback

SYMBOL GUIDE

- • Ceylon pale yellow 11/0
- | Ceylon pale gold 11/0
- o Ceylon peach 11/0
- × opaque lustered bright orange 11/0
- □ color-lined soft red 11/0
- ● transparent dark amber 11/0
- ■ iris green 11/0
- △ opaque lustered medium green 11/0
- || opaque lustered pale green 11/0

PEACH PATTERN

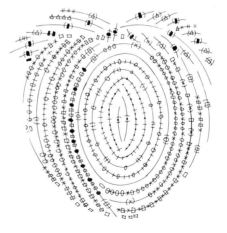

For your convenience, an enlarged version of this pattern is found on page 141.

ARCHIVAL PENDANT

ARCHIVAL PENDANT

Materials

817 metallic gold 11/0 seed beads
98 metallic gold #2 bugle beads
120 metallic gold 6/0 seed beads
14 satin-finished caramel #3 bugle beads
15 5mm x 8mm faux pearls
8" length of dark green ribbon

Photo, sticker or artwork of your choice to fit 2½" x 2" oval opening
3" x 4" bead card
3" x 4" fabric piece for backing
3" x 4" fusible webbing
1½" pinback

Directions

1. Transfer large and small oval patterns to bead card.

2. Sew lines of metallic gold 11/0 seed beads and metallic gold #2 bugle beads. Sew faux pearl on center of small oval.

3. Sew metallic gold 6/0 seed beads individually. Backtrack carefully, especially around outer edge of large oval.

4. On large oval, fuse backing fabric to stitched bead card.

5. With nail scissors, trim excess card/fabric from edges of large oval and trim excess card from small oval.

6. Trim photo, sticker or artwork to fit in center opening; glue.

7. Add 14 fringes, centered at bottom edge of large oval. Each fringe is threaded on as follows: 46 metallic gold 11/0 seed beads, one metallic gold 6/0 seed bead, one satin-finished caramel #3 bugle bead, one metallic gold 6/0 seed bead, one faux pearl and one metallic gold 11/0 seed bead. Skip last metallic gold 11/0 seed bead and run thread all the way back through other beads on fringe.

8. Tie ribbon around fringes, making a small bow about ½" below lower edge of large oval. Center and stitch small oval on top of bow.

9. Sew pinback.

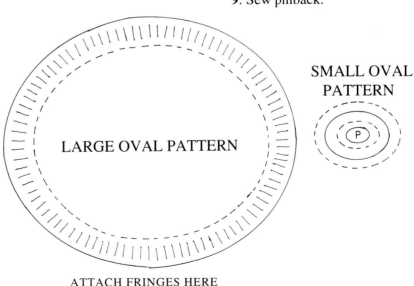

LARGE OVAL PATTERN

SMALL OVAL PATTERN

P

ATTACH FRINGES HERE

SYMBOL GUIDE

- - - - - line of metallic gold 11/0
| metallic gold #2 bugle bead
———— line of metallic gold 6/0
(P)   faux pearl

RAINBOW COMB

RAINBOW COMB

Materials

11/0 seed beads:
- 297 metallic gold
- 128 opaque lustered cream
- 32 Ceylon pink
- 30 Ceylon purple
- 77 Ceylon blue
- 20 Ceylon aqua
- 16 Ceylon green

2" x 4" bead card
2" x 4" fabric piece for backing
2" x 4" fusible webbing piece
One 2" x 2½" black hair comb
Double-sided tape

Directions

1. Transfer Rainbow pattern to bead card.

2. Outline clouds at both ends of the rainbow with metallic gold seed beads.

3. Sew lines of Ceylon blue seed beads inside clouds.

4. Fill clouds with opaque lustered cream seed beads.

5. Starting at top edge of rainbow center, sew remaining lines of beads according to pattern. Backtrack outer lines of metallic gold seed beads.

6. Fuse backing fabric to stitched bead card.

7. With nail scissors, trim excess card/fabric from edges carefully.

8. Apply double-sided tape to right side, top edge of comb.

9. Center and press beaded design firmly on top edge of comb. Secure with a few small invisible stitches. (Do not depend on tape alone to hold beading on the comb.)

SYMBOL GUIDE

- ————— metallic gold 11/0
- - - - - Ceylon aqua 11/0
- ∿∿∿ Ceylon blue 11/0
- ······· Ceylon pink 11/0
- — — — Ceylon green 11/0
- —·—·— Ceylon purple 11/0
- **(✗)** fill with opaque lustered cream 11/0

RAINBOW PATTERN

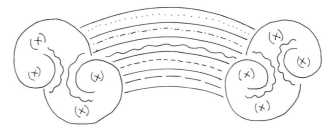

AMETHYST HAIRBUCKLE

AMETHYST HAIRBUCKLE

Materials

11/0 seed beads:
  578 metallic silver
  300 silver-lined dark amethyst
  94 lustered pale pink
  38 lustered medium pink
  54 color-lined dark rose
  104 silver-lined dark green
  160 opaque lustered light green
11/0 two-cut beads:
  110 medium green
  148 light amethyst
  142 silver-lined crystal

Eight freshwater pearls
Two turquoise chips
One 24mm round faceted acrylic flat
  stone
80 silver-lined amethyst #2 bugle
  beads
Four 6mm crystals (AB finished if
  possible)
5" x 7" bead card
5" x 7" black leather piece
5" x 7" fusible webbing piece

Directions

1. Transfer Amethyst Hairbuckle pattern on page 128 to bead card.

2. Sew metallic silver 11/0 beads. Backtrack.

3. Sew amethyst #2 bugle beads.

4. Sew freshwater pearls, turquoise chips, and 6mm crystals.

5. Sew lines of light amethyst and silver-lined crystal 11/0 two-cut beads.

6. Sew lines of opaque lustered light green 11/0 seed beads and medium green 11/0 two-cut beads.

7. Sew lines of lustered medium pink and color-lined dark rose 11/0 seed beads.

8. Fill with lustered pale pink 11/0 seed beads.

9. Fill with silver-lined dark amethyst 11/0 seed beads.

10. Fill with silver-lined dark green 11/0 seed beads.

11. Fuse leather piece to stitched bead card.

12. With nail scissors, trim excess card/leather from edges and holes carefully.

13. Glue acrylic stone in place.

To wear in hair, insert hairstick through one hole, through the hair, then out through the other hole.

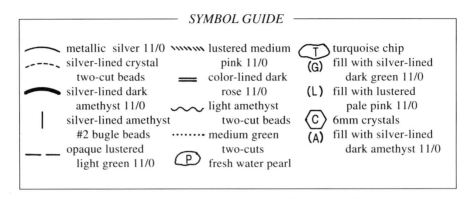

SYMBOL GUIDE

⌢ metallic silver 11/0 〰 lustered medium pink 11/0 — ⬡(T) turquoise chip (G) fill with silver-lined dark green 11/0

- - - silver-lined crystal two-cut beads ═ color-lined dark rose 11/0 (L) fill with lustered pale pink 11/0

⌒ silver-lined dark amethyst 11/0 ～ light amethyst two-cut beads ⬡(C) 6mm crystals (A) fill with silver-lined dark amethyst 11/0

| silver-lined amethyst #2 bugle beads ⋯ medium green two-cuts

– – opaque lustered light green 11/0 ⬭(P) fresh water pearl

AMETHYST HAIRBUCKLE PATTERN

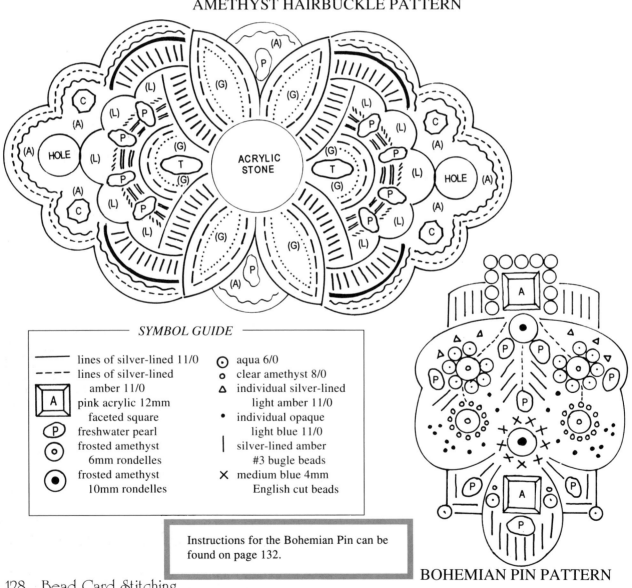

SYMBOL GUIDE

— lines of silver-lined 11/0

- - - lines of silver-lined amber 11/0

⬛(A) pink acrylic 12mm faceted square

(P) freshwater pearl

⊙ frosted amethyst 6mm rondelles

⦿ frosted amethyst 10mm rondelles

⊙ aqua 6/0

o clear amethyst 8/0

△ individual silver-lined light amber 11/0

• individual opaque light blue 11/0

| silver-lined amber #3 bugle beads

✗ medium blue 4mm English cut beads

Instructions for the Bohemian Pin can be found on page 132.

BOHEMIAN PIN PATTERN

APRIL

SUN	MON	TUES	WED	THURS	FRI	SAT
			1	2	3	4
5	6	7	8	9	10	11
12	13	14	15	16	17	18
19	20	21	22	23	24	25
26	27	28	29	30		

 PAINTBRUSH & PALETTE HAIRBUCKLE

PAINTBRUSH & PALETTE HAIRBUCKLE

Materials

All beads are glass opaque 10/0 seed beads.

159 black
258 yellow
90 lime
62 green
99 aqua
124 blue
111 purple
69 rose
85 dark orange
32 tangerine

59 red
573 metallic gold
Four Chinese turquoise chips
5" x 7" bead card
5" x 7" metallic gold leather piece for
    backing
5" x 7" fusible webbing piece
6"–8" black paintbrush or other
    suitable hairstick

Directions

1. Transfer Palette Hairbuckle pattern on page 131 to bead card.

2. Stitch outer edge in metallic gold. Backtrack.

3. Outline hole openings using opaque black.

4. Sew turquoise chips.

5. Work center checkerboard area using assorted colors as indicated on pattern.

6. Work vertical lines of gold, purple, blue and aqua in center area.

7. Work small triangular, circular and square color areas, outlining with gold where indicated.

8. Work wavy areas to left and right of center area. Fill black backgrounds where indicated.

9. Work rainbow shaded backgrounds, starting at corners with purple and adding rows of each color. Fill remainder with yellow.

10. Fuse leather piece to stitched bead card.

11. With nail scissors, trim excess card/leather from edges and holes carefully.

To wear in hair, insert hairstick through one hole, through the hair, then out through the other hole.

PALETTE HAIRBUCKLE
PATTERN

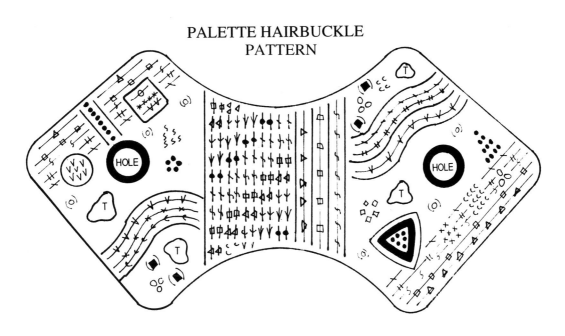

SYMBOL GUIDE

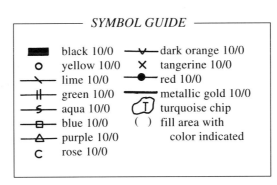

▬	black 10/0	⋎	dark orange 10/0
o	yellow 10/0	✕	tangerine 10/0
⟍	lime 10/0	●	red 10/0
‖	green 10/0	▬	metallic gold 10/0
⌇	aqua 10/0	T	turquoise chip
⊟	blue 10/0	( )	fill area with
△	purple 10/0		color indicated
C	rose 10/0		

BOHEMIAN PIN

Materials

11/0 seed beads:
    169 silver-lined light pink
    72 silver-lined light amber
    20 opaque light blue
29 aqua 6/0 seed beads
Nine medium blue 4mm English cut
    beads
26 clear amethyst 8/0 seed beads
32 silver-lined amber #3 bugle beads
One opaque aqua 10mm rondelle

One frosted amethyst 10mm rondelle
Four frosted amethyst 6mm rondelles
Two pink acrylic 12mm faceted squares
Eight freshwater pearls
2" x 3" cream satin piece
2" x 3" bead card
2" x 3" fabric piece for backing
Two 2" x 3" fusible webbing pieces
1½" pinback

Directions

1. Transfer Bohemian Pin pattern on page 128 to bead card. Retrace lines with dark ink pen; let dry.

2. Fuse webbing to wrong side of satin piece. Fuse satin directly on top of pattern on bead card; lines will show through satin well enough to bead over them.

3. Sew lines of silver-lined light pink and silver-lined light amber 11/0 seed beads.

4. Sew bugle beads.

5. Sew rondelles and acrylic squares, anchoring with silver-lined light pink 11/0 seed beads.

6. Sew freshwater pearls and English cut beads.

7. Sew aqua 6/0 seed beads, anchoring with silver-lined amber 11/0 seed beads.

8. Sew amethyst 8/0 seed beads.

9. Sew individual opaque light blue and silver-lined amber 11/0 seed beads.

10. Fuse backing fabric to stitched bead card.

11. With nail scissors, trim excess card/fabric from edges carefully.

12. Sew pinback.

BOHEMIAN PIN

VICTORIAN FLORAL BOUQUET PIN

VICTORIAN FLORAL BOUQUET PIN

Materials

11/0 seed beads:
- 245 opaque lustered light pink
- 87 color-lined medium pink
- 50 opaque dark red
- 146 opaque lustered light blue
- 86 opaque lustered medium blue
- 60 silver-lined dark aqua
- 38 opaque lustered lime
- 28 transparent rainbow medium green
- 150 iris green
- 47 lustered cream
- 31 lustered light orchid
- 24 opaque lustered medium purple
- 63 silver-lined medium gold

- 21 transparent light amethyst 6/0 seed beads
- 42 transparent light amethyst 8/0 seed beads
- 42 silver-lined gold #2 bugle beads
- One AB finished light sapphire 6mm crystal
- 4" x 4" bead card
- 4" x 4" fabric piece for backing
- 4" x 4" fusible webbing piece
- 1½" pinback

Directions

1. Transfer Victorian Floral Bouquet Pin pattern on page 136 to bead card.

2. Sew 11/0 seed beads according to pattern.

3. Sew chevron row of #2 bugle beads at lower edge of design.

4. Make fringes according to pattern.

5. Fuse backing fabric to stitched bead card.

6. With nail scissors, trim excess card/fabric from edges carefully, taking care not to cut threads.

7. Sew pinback.

VICTORIAN FLORAL BOUQUET PIN PATTERN

SYMBOL GUIDE

——— line of opaque lustered light pink 11/0

A   fill with color-lined medium pink 11/0

······· line of opaque lustered light blue 11/0

B   fill with opaque lustered medium blue 11/0

– – – line of lustered cream 11/0

C   fill with lustered light orchid 11/0

∿∿ line of opaque lustered lime 11/0

| single silver-lined gold #2 bugle bead

〰〰 line of transparent rainbow medium green 11/0

✕   single opaque dark red 11/0

□   single silver-lined dark aqua 11/0

○   single opaque lustered medium purple 11/0

△   single silver-lined medium gold 11/0

●   single iris green 11/0

⊡   iris green 11/0

⊕   silver-lined medium gold 11/0

▯   silver-lined gold #2 bugle bead

○   transparent light amethyst 8/0

○   transparent light amethyst 6/0

✪   AB finished light sapphire 6mm crystal

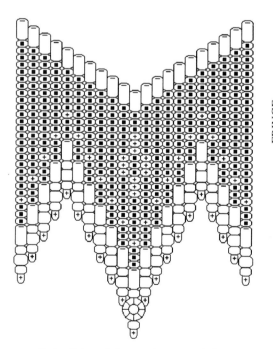

FRINGE

Note: Fringe is larger than actual size.

DOGWOOD MOSAIC PIN PATTERN

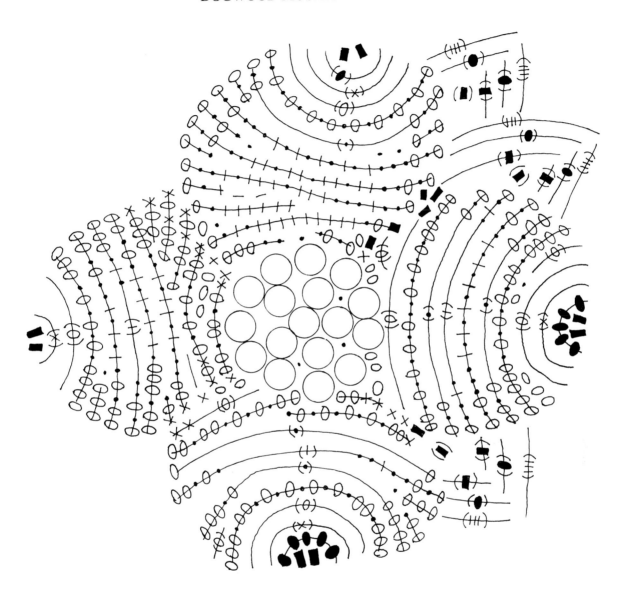

The designer has granted permission to photocopy patterns found in this book.

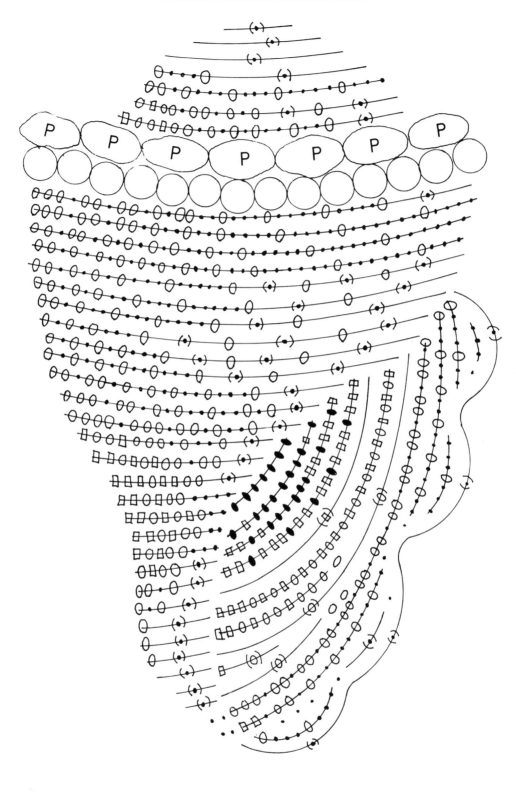

MOSAIC BRIDGE PATTERN

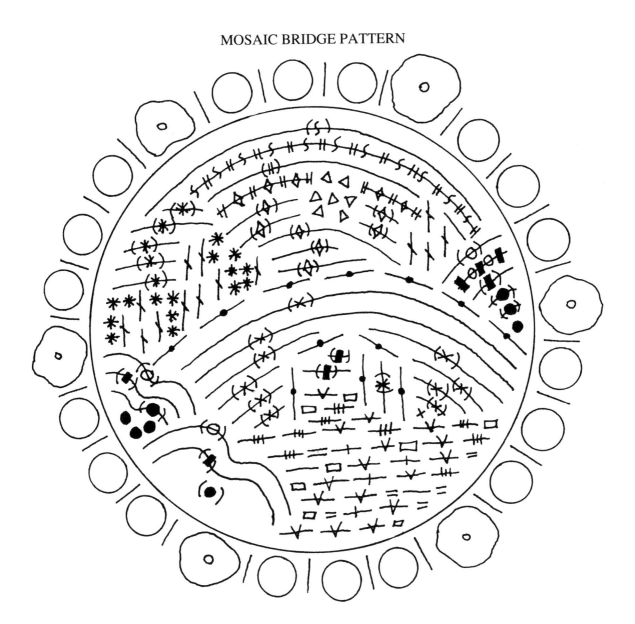

MOSAIC TREE PATTERN

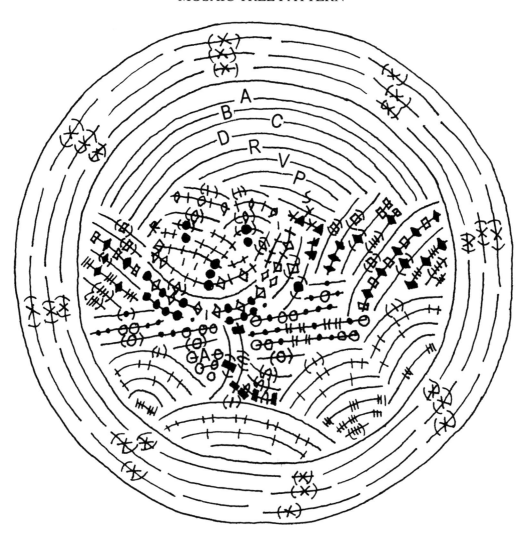

PEACH PATTERN

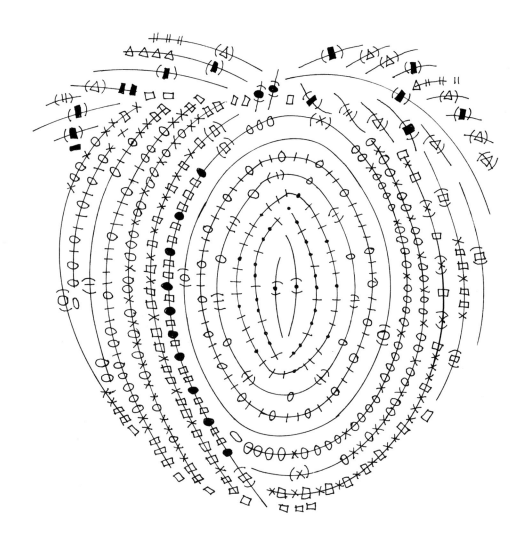

BEAD TYPES

OPAQUE solid color throughout the entire bead, usually somewhat matte in appearance, or with a dull gloss. Effective when used in Native American design.

LUSTERED either opaque or transparent, these beads have a shiny finish (sometimes gold) applied to the outside surface of the bead. Good selection of colors available; run small.

CEYLON opaque beads with a milky luminescent surface. Can appear similar to lustered beads, but slightly cloudier. Run small, with a high percentage of misshapen or irregular beads. Buy extras.

IRIS opaque beads with a slightly metallic look. Iridescent finish on the surface. Widely used because of their rich look and design versatility. Most widely used colors are green, blue and purple mixed iris. Copper, bronze and red iris are gorgeous beads, but quite costly.

RAINBOW similar to iris, but transparent. Lighter colors than metallic-look iris; can appear crystalline, almost opalescent depending on the predominant glass color.

TRANSPARENT simple glass, clear with no finish added. Tend to be irregular in size, with smaller holes. Darker colors (especially blue and green) can appear cloudy.

SILVER-LINED transparent beads of any color with the hole lined in silver. Usually available in square-holed or round-holed. Square-holed are easier to weave because the holes tend to be larger.

METALLIC beads coated with any metallic color finish. The coatings are fragile and will rub off if handled roughly. Can be badly affected by finger oils. However, if carefully handled, they are effective and beautiful.

COLOR-LINED transparent beads of any color with the hole lined in another color. The color of the outer glass will dominate. Holes can be small.

#2 BUGLES can be woven with 11 seed beads. Substitute one #2 bugle for three seed beads. Widely available in silver-lined, iris and rainbow.

#3 BUGLES are best woven by themselves because they do not fit easily with seed beads within a woven pattern. Try them as part of a fringe or hanger.

11/0 SEED BEADS are ideal for needleweaving. Can be mixed with #2 bugles.

10/0 SEED BEADS are excellent for needleweaving. Check uniformity of size.

8/0 SEED BEADS are good for use in graphic-type designs where strength is a factor.

6/0 SEED BEADS can be woven, but are heavy to wear. Try using them as embellishments on hangers or fringes.

METRIC EQUIVALENCY CHART

MM-Millimetres   CM-Centimetres

INCHES TO MILLIMETRES AND CENTIMETRES

INCHES	MM	CM	INCHES	CM	INCHES	CM
⅛	3	0.3	9	22.9	30	76.2
¼	6	0.6	10	25.4	31	78.7
⅜	10	1.0	11	27.9	32	81.3
½	13	1.3	12	30.5	33	83.8
⅝	16	1.6	13	33.0	34	86.4
¾	19	1.9	14	35.6	35	88.9
⅞	22	2.2	15	38.1	36	91.4
1	25	2.5	16	40.6	37	94.0
1¼	32	3.2	17	43.2	38	96.5
1½	38	3.8	18	45.7	39	99.1
1¾	44	4.4	19	48.3	40	101.6
2	51	5.1	20	50.8	41	104.1
2½	64	6.4	21	53.3	42	106.7
3	76	7.6	22	55.9	43	109.2
3½	89	8.9	23	58.4	44	111.8
4	102	10.2	24	61.0	45	114.3
4½	114	11.4	25	63.5	46	116.8
5	127	12.7	26	66.0	47	119.4
6	152	15.2	27	68.6	48	121.9
7	178	17.8	28	71.1	49	124.5
8	203	20.3	29	73.7	50	127.0

YARDS TO METRES

YARDS	METRES	YARDS	METRES	YARDS	METRES	YARDS	METRES	YARDS	METRES
⅛	0.11	2⅛	1.94	4⅛	3.77	6⅛	5.60	8⅛	7.43
¼	0.23	2¼	2.06	4¼	3.89	6¼	5.72	8¼	7.54
⅜	0.34	2⅜	2.17	4⅜	4.00	6⅜	5.83	8⅜	7.66
½	0.46	2½	2.29	4½	4.11	6½	5.94	8½	7.77
⅝	0.57	2⅝	2.40	4⅝	4.23	6⅝	6.06	8⅝	7.89
¾	0.69	2¾	2.51	4¾	4.34	6¾	6.17	8¾	8.00
⅞	0.80	2⅞	2.63	4⅞	4.46	6⅞	6.29	8⅞	8.12
1	0.91	3	2.74	5	4.57	7	6.40	9	8.23
1⅛	1.03	3⅛	2.86	5⅛	4.69	7⅛	6.52	9⅛	8.34
1¼	1.14	3¼	2.97	5¼	4.80	7¼	6.63	9¼	8.46
1⅜	1.26	3⅜	3.09	5⅜	4.91	7⅜	6.74	9⅜	8.57
1½	1.37	3½	3.20	5½	5.03	7½	6.86	9½	8.69
1⅝	1.49	3⅝	3.31	5⅝	5.14	7⅝	6.97	9⅝	8.80
1¾	1.60	3¾	3.43	5¾	5.26	7¾	7.09	9¾	8.92
1⅞	1.71	3⅞	3.54	5⅞	5.37	7⅞	7.20	9⅞	9.03
2	1.83	4	3.66	6	5.49	8	7.32	10	9.14

INDEX